A View of the Irish

A View of the Irish

BRIAN CLEEVE

BUCHAN & ENRIGHT, PUBLISHERS
LONDON

First published in 1983 by
Buchan & Enright, Publishers, Limited
53 Fleet Street, London EC4Y 1BE

ISBN 0 907675 17 4

Photoset in 11/12pt Plantin by
Derek Doyle & Associates, Mold, Clwyd
Printed and Bound in Great Britain by
Richard Clay (The Chaucer Press) Ltd
Bungay, Suffolk

Distributed in the USA by:
SEVEN HILLS BOOKS
CINCINNATI, OHIO

Contents

FOR TOBY AND DOMINIQUE

'The Irish are not in a conspiracy to cheat the world by false representations of the merits of their countrymen. No, Sir; the Irish are a fair people; they never speak well of one another.'

Dr Samuel Johnson, in 1775. And who is the present author to break so long-established a tradition?

Foreword

For any one man to attempt to draw a portrait of his country is a ludicrously impossible enterprise, and only a fool would undertake it. The very most he can do is to offer a random collection of opinions and say 'This is how my country appears to me.' To which any critic may answer, 'Who cares how it appears to you?'

Probably no one. My sole excuse for attempting this book is that my publishers asked me to. And when they did, I discovered that there were various things about Ireland I wanted to say. I don't claim that they are 'truths' – least of all that they are '*the* truth'. Simply that this is how these things seem to me. And where facts are concerned rather than opinions I have taken what care I could to make sure that the facts are correct. Or at least, were correct at the time of writing.

Since then, many things have happened in Ireland, as they have elsewhere. A general election has come and gone, leaving old certainties, like old reputations, in ruins. Political scandals have surfaced, to subside more in embarrassment and ridicule than in resolutions of amendment among the guilty parties. Some statistics have altered, usually, although not always, for the worse. Unemployment, an almost unbelievable 165,000 when I wrote the relevant passage, now seems likely to rise above 200,000 before the proofs are corrected. The consumption of liquor, on the other hand, has fallen, not because of Lenten repentance or New Year resolves, but simply because of the deepening depression, which has made even a pint of stout a luxury and a bottle of whiskey an investment (although smuggling has something to do with this too, smuggling liquor being a new growth industry). Nevertheless, apart from such necessarily unstable figures, I think that most of the facts I have offered in the following pages remain correct.

As for the opinions, it may appear to anyone who chances to read them that they are more carping than enthusiastic, and he or she might gather the impression that I disapprove of the country I live in. In some matters I do, and I feel that one would have to be deeply insensitive not to disapprove of many things about modern Ireland – as of many things about modern England or modern France or modern America. And when offering opinions in a book – as when offering news in a newspaper – it seems more urgent to offer the bad news rather than the blandly good. There is not a lot of point in saying 'Irish scenery is beautiful', when everyone likely to be interested knows that already. It does seem worth saying that large numbers of cretinous men with the power to do it are busy ruining as much of that beautiful scenery as they can.

And it is not only the scenery that is under threat. Of course, to a great many old men looking back with nostalgia, the past seems better than the present, and the future seems dark with the threat of one's own absence. That is not my position. A lot of Ireland's past, even her recent past, was simply awful, and desperately needed change. What is open to criticism is the direction that change has taken, and is taking, and seems likely to take tomorrow.

1 Origins and the Time Warp

Ireland is the same as England, only different. The sameness is obvious. Irish people look the same as English people, talk the same language, wear the same clothes, eat the same food, buy the same goods, live in the same kinds of houses, obey or disobey the same laws, read the same books and the same sorts of news in the same sorts of newspapers, go to the same films, watch the same TV programmes, share the same concerns in almost every area of life.

Against that solid background of sameness the difference is slight, and yet that slight difference has bewildered, maddened, infuriated or charmed English visitors to Ireland from Henry II to Mrs Thatcher. What exactly *is* the difference? And why is it there? The popular notion is that it is racial. The English are solid, stolid Saxons – 'Sassenachs' to the light-heartedly contemptuous Irish. The Irish are Celts – fey, charming, frivolous, brilliantly moody and unstable; hearty drinkers, wild fighters, tempestuous lovers; red-haired rascals courting raven-haired beauties, Errol Flynn sweeping Maureen O'Sullivan off her dainty bare feet in a little thatched cabin in Connemara, before setting off to conquer America. Gaelic Ireland yearning to be free.

One problem with this racial stereotype is that there is no agreement among its creators and holders as to what the 'Irish race' is, or looks like. Red-haired and freckled? Dark-haired and swarthy, like 'The Small Dark Man' of Maurice Walsh's pleasant novel? The slouching ape with a huge upper lip and a button nose of 19th-century *Punch* cartoons? A black-haired 'Spanish' beauty with glorious green eyes? Old Mother Riley in curlers and carpet slippers?

A second problem with the 'Celtic' theory is that it is nonsense. I remember reading somewhere that according to skull types found in graveyards there is as much 'Celtic' blood in Berkshire as there is in Wicklow. And some thirty years ago a learned investigator infuriated the professional Gaels of Ireland with a book demonstrating that the Aran Islanders, far from being examples of pure Celtic perfection, were all descended from the Cromwellian soldiers garrisoned there in the 17th century. (This attractive theory is hotly contested by P.A. O Síocháin in *Aran, Islands of Legend*, Foilsiúcháin Eireann, 1962, firstly on the grounds of the small garrison and comparatively large population, and secondly on that of how few non-Gaelic names have been recorded in Aran's subsequent history.) At about the same time a team of Norwegian scholars working on burial sites and measuring the skulls of the living inhabitants in Co. Kerry, found their 'racial' characteristics to be typically Norwegian.

No argument founded on 'race' is likely to explain anything, because even the racial term 'Celtic' is next to meaningless. 'Celtic' describes a group of languages rather than a race of people. The tall, fair-haired warriors of Celtic mythology were the chieftains and aristocracy, and the legends describing their exploits in Iron Age Ireland make it clear that they were ruling over tribes and people of a very different physical type – 'the small dark men' and 'slouching apes' of much later legends, among others. And if it is correct to describe at least the fair-haired, milk-skinned chieftains as Celts, it is equally correct to point out that almost everything about them, except their language, is identical with the Saxon chieftains who followed them into the British Isles.

The majority of the invaders of both islands would have been a random gathering of conquered clans, allied tribes, slaves, mercenaries and individual warriors who had broken away from their own tribal organisations to make their fortunes. There would have been not one but half a dozen 'races' represented. And something equally important would almost certainly have been missing – quite certainly missing from the first wave of invasion. That 'something' would have been women. The great land migrations of the Dark Ages could afford camp followers and families, protected by the locust swarm of the warriors. But when the warriors took to the sea, in small boats for long, dangerous voyages with an uncertain outcome, they left the women behind. Every hand in the boat needed to be a fighting hand. Therefore, when any invasion was successful, with the indigenous warriors defeated and driven inland, or slaughtered, the invaders included captured native women among their booty, with obvious results in half-breed children. It happened at Troy. It has happened throughout history. It must have happened in the pre-historic, 'Celtic' Ireland, or Ireland in the process of becoming Celtic.

There was certainly a substantial 'pre-Celtic' population, generally supposed to be of Mediterranean stock – the builders of such Irish monuments as New Grange and Knowth and Dowth and the other giant passage graves of the Irish Neolithic. This native population was not exterminated. Apart from the numerical unlikelihood of a handful of invaders exterminating a large settled population, there was the question of need. Need of women, as has just been mentioned. Need of peasants to provide food; craftsmen to provide new clothes, to repair weapons, to build houses; slaves, both male and female, to provide domestic services; and perhaps most important of all in the beginning, allies to act as guides and informers. Every later invasion of Ireland found allies among the existing inhabitants. It seems overwhelmingly likely that the 'Celtic' invasions – and there were several – found the same degree of co-operation.

One way or the other, it is certain that large numbers of the 'pre-Celtic' population survived, because, as has just been said, the legends and folk tales reveal their presence. More convincing still, Irish history reveals them as having survived. At the 11th-century battle of Clontarf, when a (broadly speaking) Danish-Norse federation with Irish allies fought a (broadly speaking) Irish federation with Danish-Norse allies, the latter army under Brian Boroimhe (the Brian Boru of anglicised history) included a large contingent from South-West Ireland which was recognised as being 'non-Gaelic', speaking a different language and having a different appearance from those of the other Irish contingents.

In other words, in the South-West – Kerry, West Cork, South

Limerick – the pre-Celtic population had not only survived, but had kept a form of independence, and its own language or group of languages, its own chieftains and tribal organisations. Elsewhere in Ireland these signs of independence had been lost. But that does not mean that the peoples who had once possessed them had disappeared. They would have been present in the other contingents of King Brian's army, but in the lower ranks, while the chroniclers were only interested in the chiefs. Indeed, as I write this, Conor Cruise O'Brien, of Katanga and subsequent fame, and a descendant of the great clan O'Brien of which Brian Boroimhe was once head, writes in the *Irish Times* in the course of an argument about the meaning of being Irish:

> I am Irish. I achieved this condition by being born in Ireland, of Irish parents, many of whose ancestors were in this land before the Gaels blew in, those parvenus, bringing with them their outlandish Celtic patois, and their foreign games.
> I am as autochthonous as it is humanly possible to be. I am older than the rocks among which I sit.

One section of pre-Celtic society was, it has been suggested, ancestral to the modern 'travelling people' or tinkers. There is a popular belief that they are descended from the survivors of the Famine in the 1840s, who took to the roads in the hope of finding food elsewhere. Yet the tinkers, or their equivalent, appear to have been a factor in Gaelic Ireland, not to mention Cromwellian and Penal Ireland. And there is a theory that the remote 'ancestors' of the tinkers – 'ancestors' in the social sense rather than in direct blood lineage, no doubt – were in pre-Celtic times perched precariously on the bottom rung of the social ladder, and that when the Celts arrived, they simply fell off – into a life of wandering. One possible corroboration of this theory may be found in the tinkers' hair. It is a tradition, and sometimes a fact, that tinkers have 'red' hair. More often their hair is a tawny yellow, and the colour is the result sometimes of nature, but very often of bleaching. In the old days it used to be bleached with urine, but nowadays it's done with any commercial product, or with pure ammonia. This bleaching of the hair was a habit shared in the old days with country Irish women, who also bleached their hair blonde with urine, if nature had failed them by making them dark. Now the only explanation for such a practice is that blonde hair was socially desirable, being aristocratic, whereas dark hair was inferior, the mark of the serf class. (Two thousand years ago a Chinese nobleman referred scornfully to the ordinary Chinese as the 'black-haired people', which suggests that he himself was fair, and that fair hair was 'good', black hair 'bad' and ignoble.)

The most popular explanation of the tinkers and their nomadic way of life, that they were the consequence of Cromwell's habit of massacring the bulk of the population of any captured town and herding the few wretched survivors westwards, is obviously inadequate, but it does remind me of the very curious case of the Drogheda massacre. In 1649, as is well known to every Irish man, woman and child, Cromwell's troops butchered the unfortunate inhabitants of Drogheda (among many other places).

But a friend of mine happened for some reason to be examining the municipal records of Drogheda for the exact period during which this infamous event took place. On the day before, the Town Council was discussing the inadequate state of Drogheda's street lighting. This was no doubt a necessary discussion, but it does seem an odd choice of subject with Cromwell's army camped outside the ill-lit town. Howsoever, the massacre occurred the next day, and the town records for that date are understandably blank, the Town Council evidently being unable to meet. But it did meet the day after the massacre – and continued the unfinished discussion about the street lights. Not a word about the massacre. Not so much as a passing reference to Cromwell, even in cowed flattery. Nothing. Just street lighting, pros and cons.

Why? Irish frivolity? They hadn't noticed? Because the streets were too ill-lit to see the bodies lying about? Or – more sinister – did the massacre never take place at all? Was it invented in the 19th century to add to the long list of England's actual crimes against Ireland? This is hardly likely, since the event seems well enough documented elsewhere. But not by the Drogheda Town Council, who surely had the closest interest of all, having just lost the entire body of citizenry at one blow. An odd case.

But the whole of Ireland, the entirety of Irish history, is an odd case. And yet I would suggest, with respect, that so is England, and so is English history. Just as odd. Just as full of inexplicable small mysteries and paradoxes, none of them attributable to Saxon blood, or even Norman. And all of them appearing in a subtly different light from Ireland's oddities because, in general, and until very recently, England won, and Ireland lost. A winner's oddities are accepted without anyone feeling the need for much explanation, but a loser's oddities tend to be probed to their hidden depths to explain why he lost. Nobody worries about the Duke of Wellington's foibles – he won. Every detail of Napoleon's peculiarities, from piles to eczema, has been exhaustively debated ever since he lost. I don't know why this should be so, but so it is.

Which brings me, at long last, to the why and reason of this book – why and how is Ireland different from England, if it is not a question of race? In my suggestion it is because Ireland lost and, in losing, became a poor relation, with all a poor relation's psychotic ambivalences towards its rich relation – hatred, jealousy, imitation, admiration – in endless permutations. (Whereas the rich relation, when it notices the poor relation at all, is simpler-minded – 'Dear Imelda! Such a quaint creature, but she simply adores us, I don't know why.' Or else 'That frightful creature – absolutely consumed with jealousy.' In this analogy, or imagery, the 'Dear Imelda' side is provided for by the Tom Moores and the Terry Wogans, the 'frightful creatures' side by the IRA and the Fenians and all the other revolutionaries.)

And, even more important than simply becoming a poor relation, Ireland came to occupy a different period of time to that occupied by England. This 'time-warp factor' began for Ireland in the 1st century AD, when in the international sweepstakes Britain drew the dubious first prize of Roman occupation and urban civilisation, while Ireland remained in the Iron Age, its tribal culture untouched by Roman Law or discipline or tyranny. In the 5th century AD England, under Saxon pressure, slipped back from its status as Roman province into a new barbarism, but it never slipped back as far as the point at which Ireland had remained. The Angles and Saxons soon abandoned tribalism for an attempt to reconstruct something of Roman town life, and where newly Christianised Ireland followed a non-Roman model for its Christianity, based on great abbeys set in the countryside (there being no cities) and deeply influenced by the old Druidical system, so that Irish saint and Irish druid are often indistinguishable, Saxon England followed the Roman system of bishoprics centred upon cities, with the bishops modelled on the earlier Roman Provincial governors or administrators.

Centuries later, when the Normans invaded Ireland – seven mounted men to conquer a country with a population of at least a million – the Irish were still effectively in the Iron Age, a fragmented, feud-ridden, tribal society with a surface gloss of aristocratic Christianity. Not much of a gloss either, to judge from the admittedly biased account of Giraldus Cambrensis. The Normans – no better Christians at heart, perhaps, but fine politicians with the ear of the Church of Rome bent attentively towards them – were several hundred years in advance of the Irish. They had good, heavy cavalry horses, stirrups, saddles with high-built horns fore and aft for stability when fighting from horseback, and complete body armour, the equivalent of tanks fighting almost naked tribesmen. With Irish allies and Welsh auxiliaries, seven such horsemen proved enough.

The mention of stirrups brings a curious fact to mind. The stirrup seems to have been invented in the Byzantine Empire around the 6th century AD and to have reached Western Europe within the next three hundred years. The Normans brought it to Leinster at least, the easternmost province of Ireland, in the 12th century, but five centuries later it was still almost unknown in Gaelic Ireland, west of the Shannon.

More surprising still, the horse collar, first known and used in central Europe about the year 700 AD had not become an accepted fact of life in the far west of Ireland 1,000 years later. The English garrison of Galway city kept an official whose main task was to prevent the local peasantry from 'ploughing by the tail' – in other words hitching the plough to the horse's tail, a practice which resulted inevitably in pulling the wretched creature's tail off at the root. (The English concern was not mainly animal welfare. Horses were valuable to the community for ploughing and providing food, and were also useful in warfare, when the law allowed that they could be commandeered. Horses with their tails pulled off, even if they survived the injury, were practically useless, and certainly shameful for English soldiers to ride.)

· The man who reported on Connemara's ploughing – an adventurous bookseller attempting to sell English bibles to the natives, a kind of Livingstone of his day – underlined in all his letters from the west of Ireland, and indeed from the whole of Ireland, the time lapse I have mentioned. In 17th-century Connemara a Gaelic chieftain could organise an entire countryside for a stag hunt, as his ancestors had done for two thousand years; in his valley, nothing had greatly changed during that time. In England at the same moment Newton was abandoning alchemy for science; London was becoming a major city; the Royal Society was stimulating a generation of true scientists; the agricultural revolution was soon to begin, and in its turn to make possible the Industrial Revolution, by providing surpluses of cheap food for new towns and factories. None of this touched Ireland.

A hundred and fifty years later Ireland suffered the worst famine of its history (there had been an almost equally terrible one in the 1740s) because the poorest peasantry of the west and south depended wholly and solely upon one crop, potatoes. The turnip, and other root vegetables which had transformed the English working-class diet, were unknown in the west of Ireland where the Famine hit hardest. (It is still hard for the visitor to find a good range of vegetables in the west of Ireland and in many country towns the shopkeeper will excuse the absence of vegetables by explaining that the lorry hasn't yet arrived from Dublin.) And, thinking of the Famine, it has often been pointed out that the Irish starved while surrounded by a sea full of fish, and a coast rich in lobsters, crabs, crayfish, mussels, winkles, whelks and all the riches of a rich sea-shore. The Irish simply looked at their dying potatoes and died with them. They had no boats, most of them, no knowledge of fishing, no experience of any other food but potatoes, no natural leaders they trusted except their clergy, who in practical matters were not much better than their illiterate parishioners. Of course, one must qualify this picture in many ways, and no one should conclude from it that the Famine was the 'fault' of its victims. But ignorance was an important factor, even if wheat was being exported from Ireland to England throughout the Famine years.

So much for the agricultural revolution of 'Turnip' Townsend and his like. The Industrial Revolution made scarcely a greater impact on

Ireland. Railways appeared, and a few metalled roads near Dublin; gas light came to Dublin and Cork, as it had to London and Bristol; coal replaced turf as fuel in wealthy homes; here and there bathrooms made a shy appearance. But not factories, not anything equivalent to England's growing industrial class, England's new industrial towns. There were no mines, no shipyards – except an embryonic one in Belfast, a city soon to become the only near equivalent to an English industrial town.

Ireland remained firmly stuck in the 18th century as far as Dublin and the 'civilised' east were concerned, and in a still remoter epoch in the far south and west. When disdainful English visitors arrived to lift scornful eyebrows at Irish 'backwardness' and general Paddy-whackery, what they were looking at was not peculiarly or uniquely Irish. It was very similar to what England had been a hundred or two hundred or five hundred years earlier.

The savage faction fights that were the Irish equivalent of modern football hooliganism on Saturdays – and undoubtedly they were savage, for a Limerick surgeon claimed to have more experience of head injuries than any medical man in Europe. He always attended the victims of such affairs, and indeed wrote a best-selling book on the subject in the early 19th century – these faction fights should be compared not to the Sunday School behaviour of 19th-century English cities, but to the behaviour of London mobs in the previous century, or to the clan warfare in Scotland a hundred years earlier still. The 19th-century faction fights were tribal affairs, but by then no longer conducted with swords and spears and battle-axes, but with sticks. (And a heavy Irish stick with a good, solid, fist-sized knob on the end could be a fearsome weapon in the right – or wrong – hands. The shillelagh, however, so named from the famous Shillelagh oak woods, last remnant of Ireland's primeval forests that once covered the whole country, is a pure invention for tourists, designed to encourage them to buy itty-bitty sticklets varnished black and painted with shamrocks.)

Oddly enough, the one solid impact the English Industrial Revolution made upon Ireland was in religion. The peculiarly puritanical nature of Irish Catholicism (and I am not sure that it is peculiar to Ireland. Italian and Spanish Catholicism, at least for the peasantry, is surely equally puritanical?) is often ascribed to the influence of Jansenism, the reasoning being that during the Penal days of the 18th century, when Irish priests were barred from being trained at home, aspiring priesteens went off to France to be trained and ordained and there fell under French Jansenist influence, an influence which they brought back to Ireland. Thus, when the Irish seminary of Maynooth was founded by English permission in 1795, the French influence remained, through Irish bishops earlier trained in France and through refugee French priests escaped from the Revolution in their own country.

All this may well be true, but a far more significant influence upon Irish religion was English middle-class Victorian piety, itself the product of the Industrial Revolution. The English middle classes and employing classes used God to tame the beast in their servants and employees – and in their wives and children – and the Catholic priesthood of Ireland, yearning itself to be respectably middle-class and to imitate the factory-rich English relation, imported the same type of urban piety into rural Ireland. If parishioners tried to insist upon retaining an 18th-century gaiety, the parish priest was determined that they should not. Not because gaiety was immoral, or un-Christian, but because it was not respectable. It let down the Catholic image. It was backward. And so, at much the same time that Protestant missionaries were dressing Tahitian girls in Mother Hubbards, and trying to explain to them that sex was wrong, the Catholic priests of Ireland were doing much the same for their own bewildered flocks.

The sexual habits of any population are always too varied to be captured by statistics, but it does seem true that whereas peasant marriages in Ireland before the middle of the 19th century tended to occur when both partners were still in their teens (in spite of some evidence to the contrary provided by Brian Merriman's long poem, *The Midnight Court*, dealing with the reluctance of Irish bachelors to get married at all), after about 1850 a practice of late and very late marriages set in, with the husband likely to be well into his thirties and the bride in her late twenties.

Some of this can be ascribed to the effects of the Famine on those survivors who remained in Ireland. They were rightly terrified of bringing a clatter of children into a world that might not feed them, and to put off marriage for ten or twelve years was an effective form of birth control. But the influence of the Church reinforced that of the Famine. Sex and hilarity were out, and a muffling, black-suited, black-gloved, top-hatted respectability was in. Neither were outward signs of Irishness necessarily respectable. O'Connell the Liberator, himself a native Irish speaker, had told his followers in the 1820s and 1830s that if they wanted to be successful like the English they must stop talking Irish, and learn the language of the landlord. In the 1850s the priests told their followers – the sons of O'Connell's followers – that if they wanted to be even half as successful as the English they must stop fornicating in the hedges of a Saturday night. And to make sure they stopped, the parish priest would arm himself with a sturdy blackthorn stick and go round his hedge-ridden parish, routing out offenders with heavy thwacks where it would hurt most.

All this passion for respectability was deliberate policy on the part of the Irish hierarchy, as it had been with O'Connell. Unless the Irish became like the English, they could never succeed, nor count for anything in the world. And unless Irish Catholics became like English Protestants, they would never count for anything either, and the Church would be the loser. The hierarchy longed for recognition, for status, for the esteem of authority, and how can one achieve any of that if one's ignorant followers are rabbiting away in every ditch from Donegal to Waterford? The ideal was to be Dr Bowdler and Mrs Grundy, united in middle-aged matrimony, with a Sacred Heart and a crucifix casting a chastening gloom over the marriage bed. (At about the same time in England, Jane Austen's favourite niece was deciding that Aunt Jane had been lamentably coarse. And the right-thinking bourgeoisie were putting skirts on piano legs.)

Respectability! Make the Irish respectable! Put them in button boots and broadcloth! Purge their minds! Tame their passions! These were the heart cries of every sort of authority in Ireland, from the Viceroy to the lowliest curate and schoolmaster. Magistrates set themselves to stop the Irish killing each other in faction fights. Father Mathew, founder of the first Irish Total Abstinence Association in 1838, set out to stop them drinking themselves to death with illicit whiskey, the poteen from the private stills that dotted every parish. (In this laudable endeavour his chief financiers and supporters were the legalised whiskey distillers, who didn't mind the Irish getting drunk, but minded very much if they did so without contributing to the distillers' profits.)

The Church also laid a heavy hand on the Irish language, seen as a handicap in the effort to attain respectability. English-speaking priests were sent to Irish-speaking parishes; children were severely punished for speaking Irish, even by their own Irish-speaking parents. Irish was backwardness, ignorance, while English was progress, and a hearty taste of the strap for the children who failed to learn this lesson. But the Irish tongue was not only backward, it was coarse, vulgar, its literature unreadable for a respectable man – and unthinkable for a woman.

By the 1870s and '80s this attitude of mind had had such an effect that Gaelic culture was dead, killed by authority. The language was still shamefacedly muttered by handfuls of peasants too ignorant or too obstinate to abandon it. But it was no longer written, as it had been for fourteen hundred years, celebrating love and sex and springtime, praising girls with breasts like white milk and lips like blood on the snow. None of that was respectable, and Queen Victoria would have hated it, if she had ever heard about it. A famous, and justly famous, Irish archbishop, Dr MacHale, did his best to reverse the process and rekindle love of the language, by writing many tracts in it. But he had been brought up speaking English, and the Irish he wrote is a translation from English rather than the real article.

But just as the corpse of the culture was being laid out for burial, new visitors arrived at the wake. These were the middle-class nationalists. They half agreed with the murderers that the dead creature had deserved to die. She had not been respectable. But she had been beautiful. Suppose – suppose that out of her grave there should rise a new Gaelic culture, that *was* respectable? Pure, chaste, fit for the most exacting Victorian drawing room? And so these enthusiasts – and they *were* enthusiasts, filled with an idealism that, however misty-eyed and sometimes ill-conceived, should shame most of us today – these enthusiasts set off on foot or by bicycle to restore and re-create the culture so recently and venomously massacred. They collected folk tales and folk songs and folk music and folk speech. They worshipped the simple because the simple were pure of heart and purely Irish. They dressed in Irish tweeds and Irish brogues and carried Irish walking-sticks as they tramped the boreens of the West, drenched in the gentle Atlantic mists and downpours.

Anyone who loves Ireland owes these men and women a debt that can never be paid. They did it for love, and nothing else, for no one paid them. In their lifetime no one admired them or praised them. Since their deaths, often in abject poverty and neglect, no one but a handful of scholars and enthusiasts has remembered them. That much of Irish culture and Irish language survives is because of these wandering scholars and revivalists. May the earth rest lightly on their bones. And if they had the faults of their period, a passion for respectability that interfered with their scholarly and cultural aims, so that what they revived was not truly the same as what had died, who can throw stones at them? Above all not us, who have revived nothing, and have let their work decay again into gravedust.

But if one admires and loves and pays tribute to the revivalists, it is not unjust to their memory to point out that though they themselves were Irish, the nature of what they were doing was not at all peculiar to Ireland. Similar enthusiasts were at work in every country of Europe, from Finland to Sicily, from Brittany to Greece, doing the same things for the same purpose – to rescue the last remnants of pre-industrial culture before they disappeared for ever. Ireland's triumph over England, and it is a very small one, is that Irish scholars (with some admirable English and continental ones to help them) set about this revival with far greater thoroughness and success than did English scholars with the same work in England. The result is that Irish pre-industrial culture seems much richer and stronger, more 'Celtic' and 'other worldly', than its English equivalent, reinforcing the stereotypes of Irish feyness and mysticism and English phlegmatic stolidity. But if what has been irretrievably lost in England had been equally well recorded before it finally disappeared, we would have a different and more balanced picture. There can be no doubt in the world that England's peasant culture was once just as rich and strange as Ireland's, and if one is to find real differences between England and Ireland they do not lie in that culture.

And now, having said a few complimentary things about the Irish Revival Movement, it is necessary to offer the other side of the coin. The movement, in spite of its idealism, was largely false, and wholly doomed, in part because it was also wholly middle-class in inspiration, leaving the working-class untouched. Of course, here and there working men and women learned Irish, and working-class children were taught Irish dances, but that was as far as it went.

Worse still for the future, its effect was separatist and backward-looking. Its deliberate aim was to cut off Ireland's intellectual life from England's, even though England was the nearest and best and almost only source of real intellectual stimulus. It was also a further turning-back into the past, and this time not even a real past, but a manufactured, invented past, based on 19th-century misconceptions and expurgations of 18th- and 17th- and 16th-century realities. It was as though William Morris and the pre-Raphaelites had gained not only cultural but political significance in England. For here was the heart of the problem. The Gaelic revivalists became politicians, albeit often against their will and inclination. But it happened, inevitably. Political nationalism and the Cultural Revival Movement became one and the same.

And as always happens in such cases, it was not the pure scholars and enthusiasts who survived. They were shouldered aside by more equivocal, ambitious figures. By politicians using the culture, rather than loving and understanding it. It was this middle-class, urbanised Gaelic culture movement that was to inspire the Irish Revolutions of 1916 to 1921, and to control and shape them, as it would also control and shape the new Irish Free State and its successor Republic for forty years. While England advanced faster and faster, if with a somewhat unsteady gait, into the 20th century, Ireland stayed firmly in the 19th, fast in the grip of Dr O'Bowdler and Mrs MacGrundy,* well shod in galoshes, well wrapped in strong flannel underwear (known as passion killers), and armed with stout umbrellas for protection against foreign thoughts.

For a brief period before 1916 the future attempted to gain a foothold in Ireland, in the shape of Marxist socialism as interpreted by the Trade Union leaders James Connolly and Jim Larkin. But Connolly came to an abrupt end in Kilmainham Gaol after the Easter Rising of 1916, and by then Larkin was already in America,

---

* Irish cousins of Scotland's Dr Thomas Bowdler – famous as the expurgator of Shakespeare (hence 'to bowdlerise') – and of England's Mrs Grundy – an offstage character in Thomas Morton's play, *Speed the Plough*, who has passed into the language as a symbol of evangelical rectitude.

tarnished by scandal. The faint 'threep-threep' of a Socialist dawn chorus was drowned by the nationalist uproar of 'The Soldier's Song', and the clatter of middle-class boots kicking their way to the new troughs created by independence in 1921 – 'Get out of my way, damn you, Murphy, before I tread on your ugly, working-class face.'

Victorian respectability had triumphed, just as it was receiving its death blow in England from the Bright Young Things and the Roaring Twenties. While Young England learned to drink cocktails and bob its hair, Young Ireland retired, or was dragged by its elders, behind the shamrock curtain, lovingly and carefully woven for us by the Nationalists and the clergy during the latter part of the 19th century.

2 The Irish Free State

A pious respectability was the watchword for the New Ireland of the 1920s and '30s as it had been for mid-19th-century Ireland. The ideal Free State Citizen – Sean Citizen to his masters in the new parliament, Dáil Eireann – the ideal citizen was a daily communicant and a total abstainer, who spent his evenings attending classes in the Irish language. The ideal citizeness was 'Mother of Ten', a frequent writer of indignant Letters to the Editor, giving out about the disgrace of young gerruls showing their knees at dances.

Knees were a constant source of anxiety. If female children went to school in short skirts, nuns would pin newspapers round the hem as a protection for the minds of fellow seven-year-olds. Dances were another perennial worry for the clergy. 'Late dancing' of a Saturday evening – that is, a dance running past midnight and into the smallest hours of Sunday – needed the permission of the local bishop before the Civic Guards would grant a licence. Most bishops knew their duty and refused permission.

Eamon de Valera – when at last he got into power as Prime Minister (Taoiseach) in 1932 – croaked sombrely of lissom lads and comely maidens dancing jigs and reels at the crossroads in every parish, presumably in a wholesome daylight. But this idyll was no more to be contaminated by the 20th century than was any other aspect of Irish life. The ideal youngster not only danced jigs and reels in preference to the foxtrots of across the Irish Sea (not to speak of the unspeakable, such as the Charlestons and Black Bottoms from across the Atlantic). The same youngster played hurling instead of hockey and Gaelic football instead of Association, oblivious of the historical fact that so-called Gaelic football was introduced into Ireland by the rough and brutish English soldiery during the Middle Ages. For a young man to play Rugby (invented by an Irish boy from Clonmel) was to cut himself off from the well-springs of the Nation and mark him out as a West Briton – than which no accusation could be more terrible, despite the impeccably Celtic nature of the word 'Briton'. (Oddly enough the word Eire, chosen for the new state, appears to be non-Celtic, or so most scholars agree.) Girls were to play Camogie (a feminine version of hurling in which it was supposedly forbidden for the girls, unlike the boys, to kill one another) and if these excitements, added to the jigs and reels, were not enough, there were Feis Ceoil (music festivals), in which youngsters of both sexes, decently separated from one another and in the presence of their mothers, sang their little hearts out about the beauties of Eire, and danced their little toes off to please de Valera.

To protect their Gaelic innocence from Sassenach lubricity, however, there had to be censorship. Foreign books, films, and newspapers – especially Sunday newspapers – were subjected to Dr O'Bowdler's closest scrutiny. Ideally, all such imports would have been banned utterly, along with artificial means of contraception, but this is an imperfect world, and failing an outright ban there was, from 1930 onwards, censorship. Among the books the axe fell with pious fervour on any novel in which men and women made love or even thought about it with less than total delicacy. From Plato to Netta Muskett, the horrid imports were sent scurrying back across the Irish Sea.

Among films, the salacious laxness of the Hollywood Hayes code, under which men and women could actually kiss on a bed if the man was fully dressed and had one foot on the floor (as in billiards) – that fearful toleration of evil was sternly corrected, so that Tarzan, instead of shouting 'Me man, you woman!' would be confined to saying 'Me man!', shaking his head in innocent bewilderment about the queer non-man creature in front of him.

Cinema posters were another source of deep concern, often in their original state revealing that women had breasts. These were painted out vigorously with good Gaelic black paint, so that some film stars were made to look as if they had had nasty accidents and been given first aid with black bandages. Their skirts were often lengthened as well, particularly those of young ladies in Stone Age or forest costume, like Tarzan's Jane. (The same delicate concern was shown for the wax models of young ladies in shop windows. Woe betide the careless window dresser who revealed the intimacies of his statuesque charges as he changed their winter woollies for spring outfits. Mother of Ten, innocently passing such a dreadful display, would faint on the pavement, and have to be revived with brandy before she was strong enough to complain to the manager and write to the papers about it.)

As has been said, Sunday newspapers were a particular concern of Eire's moral guardians. The very tit-bits that delighted Irish building workers in Coventry or Birmingham were considered mental poison for their brothers and sisters at home in Ballyboreen. Woe betide the paper that tried to tell Ireland about the vicar who stole the choir-mistress's knickers and flew them from his church steeple. That paper would be sent back whence it came, unsold and unread, at a sad loss to the owners. Accordingly, Fleet Street learned to apply self-censorship, producing 'Irish' editions in which all scandalous tales would be replaced by innocent stories such as 'Irish pigeon wins English race' – a news item to warm even de Valera's heart.

Ireland's moral safety thus assured from English attack, the other two great concerns of the thirties – and forties and fifties – were religion and the language. The ideal was not only 'Ireland free, a nation once again', but Ireland free from sin and speaking Irish. The infant telephone directory became studded with the new Irish versions of old English names – Smith becoming MacGabhann, Brown becoming de Brún, Jones becoming Heaven knows what. Men and women – usually men – whose ancestors had dropped the O and the Mac from their names in the interests of respectability, now put them back in the same interest.

In some schools *all* subjects were taught through Irish, with the predictable result that generations of children grew up with only a very shaky grasp of either language, and not much grasp at all of anything else except the Catechism. This of course, the Church having its head screwed firmly on the right way round, was almost always taught through English, and pounded into tiny sinners for many hours each week, day after day. 'Now my lad, how do we define the Divine Mercy?' 'I don't know, sir.' 'You don't know, you atheistical little villain? By the Holy, I'll teach you how to define the Divine Mercy! Take that, curse ye, and that and that!' Thwack, thwack, scream, scream, and another lost soul saved for Paradise.

The knowledge that five times out of six the small saved sinner would have to emigrate to hated England in order to avoid starvation was a neglected fact of life in Irish education. So long as he or she went to England with a firm knowledge of the Divine Mercy and a smattering of Irish, the rest was up to God.

I say smattering, because the fact is that the revival of the Irish language as a living language never became reality. Broadly speaking, there are two reasons why this is the case. Firstly, very few children wanted to learn it – their parents did not speak it, nor did anyone use it in ordinary life. It had neither social prestige nor reason to back it up, and except in the Irish Civil Service and the public service, it did not lead to employment. To the ordinary child it seemed a totally pointless and hideously sadistic exercise. No earthly purpose would ever be served by knowing Irish, except some purpose arbitrarily invented by the same adult sadists who caned and strapped a child into learning the language. To tell a pupil that Irish was 'necessary' for entry into the Civil Service, for example, was simply one more cruel joke at the child's expense. Irish was no more *necessary* there than anywhere else. It was simply a pretence, like everything else to do with the language.

The second rock on which the revival foundered was the quality of teachers. In a great many national schools, it was a case of the semi-literate teaching the illiterate. Very few teachers of Irish had a firm grasp of that language, and even where they knew the grammar well enough to teach it properly, they were unlikely to have any real appreciation of its potential in creating beauty. And such appreciation as they did have was strangled by that all pervading respectability, that MacGrundyism that had survived in Ireland from the depths of Victorian hypocrisy.

Of course these facts were not acknowledged. Hordes of civil servants and national school teachers, armed with bicycle clips and Dineen's *Dictionary of the Irish Language*, pedalled westward every summer to the Gaeltachtaí of the West, or the South-West, or the North-West, to perfect their book-learned Irish at the feet of the only true heirs of the great days of the Gael, the illiterate or semi-literate peasantry and fisher folk of the small and ever-shrinking areas where Irish was still the natural, native speech. (Tiny money allowances were granted to Gaeltacht families on condition that they never spoke English, and Irish government inspectors were much hated for trying to trap the children into speaking a few words of English, so that the allowance could be withheld.)

Gently amazed native Irish speakers would receive these city enthusiasts and agree to teach them the pure milk of Gaeldom. But here several problems arose. Each Gaelic-speaking area had its own dialect, and the differences between one dialect and another were often so great that they were mutually incomprehensible. A teacher of Irish who perfected his knowledge of the language in Donegal would return to Dublin to teach a language that, even if perfectly learned, would not be clearly understood in Connemara or Kerry.

Worse still, as the language was written in new books, whether for teaching or entertainment, these differences not only remained but were consecrated and even exaggerated. Each dialect had its fierce defenders, who regarded their version as the only truly Irish one. Children who had the misfortune to begin learning Irish under, say, a 'Kerry' teacher, and then to pass on into the care of a 'Donegal' teacher a year or so later, found themselves utterly at sea.

To confound confusion, the authorities began changing the written language, substituting breath marks for Hs, one variety of spelling for another, and so on and so on – so much so that the title of an Irish book that has been re-issued in several editions may find itself spelled differently four or five times over in the catalogues.

But most of all and worst of all, from the point of view of anyone with a real care for the ancient culture, the new masters of the Irish Free State had no such care. They were, by and large, lower-middle-class vandals, hobbledehoys, yobs, yahoos, whose idea of art was a plaster statue. (When the same class of people erected a statue of St Patrick on the Hill of Tara, they had it cast in cement.) It is not possible to teach a love of anything if you do not possess such a love, and the new masters did not love Gaelic culture. They simply hoped to use it, for political ends or professional advancement. There grew up a gruesome caste of people who were professional Gaels, men with egg-stained waistcoats who used the language as their parents had used manure forks. They not only failed to love Gaelic culture; they sometimes seemed to have an active hatred for it. The few fine writers of Irish who existed were neglected, or reduced to translating worthless English books into Irish, while their own manuscripts gathered dust year after year in the State Publishing House, awaiting publication.

Those writers of worth who did get published saw their works fall into the lifeless hands of readers who had no critical faculties, but who would simply read anything if it was in Irish. And even such readers were pitifully few. The late and great Máirtín Ó Cadhain, whom those who should know have compared to Tolstoy, said that there were only 600 people in Ireland who could really understand the dialect in which he wrote.

Of course, all this is a wretchedly biased picture, which will be bitterly rejected by the first Irish speaker you may happen to meet. But just as the old saying went – 'If you're so clever why aren't you rich?' – so one could say, 'If the Revival Movement is so wonderful, why isn't everyone speaking Irish?' Outside the Gaeltachtaí no one speaks Irish except a very few people as a self-conscious and largely middle-class exercise. In the Gaeltachtaí almost everyone can speak English, and more and more of them speak it for preference, because English is the language of employment. The Gaeltachtaí are shrinking year by year, and where Irish is still spoken, it is spoken less and less richly, year by year. Periodically the Irish Revival organisations insist upon a national survey, intended to discover people's attitudes to the language, but these surveys are always so worded that a favourable response is inevitable. Who, in Ireland's general climate of tolerant hypocrisy, is likely to declare himself or herself 'against the language revival'? Moreover, it is nicely heartwarming to tell the eager-faced young enquirer that one speaks the language every day, even though one hasn't used ten words of it since one thankfully left school twenty years ago. And most people haven't spoken Irish, and never did, and never will.

Irish was not only a compulsory subject in the Irish Leaving Certificate, but also the only one in which failure meant failure of the whole exam. Nearly a third of all school hours were devoted to it. All this should have resulted in something at least approaching bilingualism. But it has done nothing of the kind. A few years ago the rules were relaxed to the extent that Irish was no longer compulsory in the Leaving Certificate, though its teaching at school remained compulsory. And the truth is that this was the only universally popular amendment to Irish educational rules since 1921.

But every nation has its sacred cows, which amuse other nations no end. It would be rude for a foreigner to suggest that there exists any English equivalent to the Irish Language Revival, but perhaps English readers can supply the lack for themselves. Meanwhile, Sean Citizen and Maire Citizeness spent the first forty years of the new State's existence thinking of many other things besides the Irish language and Gaelic culture. And these things, muffled though they were in the green swathes of O'Bowdlerism and MacGrundyism, were so similar to the things occupying English minds during the same period that it is not worth recounting them. There were jobs first of all – preferably something 'permanent and pensionable' in the Civil Service. There was the Depression. There was the Second World War, known in Southern Ireland as the Emergency, and during which a great many Irish people of ultra-nationalist leanings were mildly glad to see the English having a tough time. But a very great many, whatever their thoughts, volunteered for the British services. In proportion to population, more joined from the South than from the ultra-patriotic North. In the First World War, 300,000 volunteered from the South, and between 39,000 and 40,000 were killed. In the Second World War there were 183,000 volunteers from the twenty-six counties, and while no figures seem to exist for the number killed, ten Southern Irishmen and one Northern Catholic won Victoria Crosses. But no war memorial exists in the South to those who fell in the Second World War, and no general commemoration is ever held for those who fell in either war; 'Poppy Day' does not exist today in Southern Ireland. It is as if those many dead had never died – a sad comment on Irish provincial-mindedness. Many battles seemed to be fought largely by Irish troops and Irish generals. Perhaps that is why the British kept losing until 1942, although, to be strictly fair, when given the chance English generals did just as badly.

After the war-cum-emergency, emigration, which had been

increasing yearly during the '30s, became a flood, a haemorrhage. By the early 1960s something over a million Irish-born people were living in England. (One wonders what would have happened if they had all had to stay at home? Socialism? Fascism? Anarchy?) It is a proof of the first contention in this book, that Irish people are the same as English people, that this enormous immigration into England passed almost unnoticed. The newcoming Irish fitted into the pattern of English life without a hiccup. Indeed, from the immigrants' point of view the transfer was often easier between Ireland and England than it would have been between one part of Ireland and another – a Dubliner, for instance, could fit into London much easier than he could into Cork. And there was work in England, and wages, and the Welfare State, with its National Health, and an unexpurgated *News of the World*. It was beginning to be hard to find reasons to stay in Ireland.

Then came the sixties proper, swinging in London, and almost as revolutionary in Ireland. Mini-skirts arrived to give final cardiac arrest to Mother of Ten and poor O'Bowdler. The Censorship Board was drastically reformed, and Plato and Netta Muskett and several thousand other less deserving authors were restored to grace, including every distinguished living Irish writer, from Sean O'Faolain to Kate O'Brien. Indeed, not to have been banned, so that now one could be unbanned, was a kind of stigma. (Since then the Irish critics have taken over from the censors, ensuring that though Irish writers may now see their books circulated in Ireland, they won't enjoy it.)

Tower blocks were built, to replace the tedious Georgian terraces that the English had ruthlessly imposed on a subject nation, and that for obscure reasons weird foreigners enjoyed so much. Computers made a timid first appearance, and transistor radios, and vodka, and television. Men and women, boys and girls, began to drink in pubs together, and go to bed together afterwards, without benefit of clergy. And too often without benefit of contraception, so that to replace the emigrant flood into England, by then dying to a trickle, there began a steady stream of pregnant girls, hoping for a National Health abortion, or a Liverpool quicky.

De Valera's puritan approach to economics was replaced by Sean Lemass's more pragmatic style. What counted now was profit. The ideal Irishman was no longer O'Bowdler but O'Clore, the property developer. New factories, new houses, new roads – at long last Ireland was going to catch up with England and occupy not only the same century but the same decade. Even the problem of partition was going to be solved, because Southern Ireland was to become so prosperous that Northern Ireland would beg to be admitted. The Southern and Northern prime ministers met one another and cautiously shook hands. (One of the Northern PM's predecessors had vowed that no patriotic Ulsterman could employ a Catholic, which vow did not prevent him from visiting the South incognito for the shooting. Presumably Catholic kitchenmaids were flushed out of coverts by Protestant beaters, to be gunned down by Himself?) By 1968 Utopia was round the corner, and Irish architects were poised to build it in the worst possible modern style.

At which point arose the Civil Rights Movement in the North, to the mutual horror of politicians, North and South. To understand what happened then, and what has followed since, one needs to back-track fifty years, as so often in Irish events, to the effective beginnings of the Irish Republican Army and the modern Republican movement. Just before the First World War there were two opposing forces at work in Irish revolutionary circles. One was working-class and Marxist, and the other middle-class and Nationalist, as has already been said. At Easter 1916 both forces joined together, in spite of the misgivings of the Marxists. The misgivings were justified: their one real leader, Connolly, was executed; their strength was decimated; their role was taken over by the Nationalists and perverted to the benefit of bourgeois nationalism. The result was that the flowering of Socialism in Ireland proved pathetically short-lived, despite the fact that a 'soviet' of workers and peasants which set up a 'republic' in Limerick in 1919 was the first to be established outside Russia. The shooting by British soldiers of a prisoner on hunger strike sparked off the incident, and for a brief period Limerick stood in the world limelight. A general strike was called in the city, and the Committee was soon printing money, permits, lists of food prices and a citizens' bulletin. Even the Bishop of Limerick pledged his support, criticising the repressive measures taken by the British. But before long he, for one reason or another, changed his mind, and the soviet received another body-blow soon afterwards when the railway unions decided against giving their support. And so the Limerick republic died, strangled by a combination of Church, British Army and conservative trade unions. (The soviet sent a telegram to Lenin asking for help. He failed to reply.) Further flickerings of Socialism occurred in the years 1921–3, at Knocklong in Cork, in Co. Clare and elsewhere in south-western Ireland, but these embers of change flared but briefly, before being doused by the Irish Farmers' Union and the military.

The Irish Republican Army was born in January 1919 out of the earlier Irish Volunteer movement, founded in 1913 in answer to an apparently threatening Protestant para-military organisation. The Irish Volunteers split a year later, in 1914, into two factions, the moderate majority becoming the National Volunteers and the more radical and partly Marxist minority retaining the name Irish Volunteers. This opposition of two tendencies, one middle-class and nationalist, one working-class/intellectual and Marxist, continued into the IRA in 1919 and thereafter, to have its most notorious result in the split between the Official (Marxist) IRA and the Provisional (Nationalist) IRA in 1970. (But since nothing is ever left that simple the Provisional IRA now contains a powerful, perhaps dominant working-class and semi-Marxist element.) By 1924 the IRA was solidly middle-class (even if a Marxist tendency did still remain within it like a hidden root, waiting to burst into flower forty years later). The IRA's typical recruit was an ardent Catholic, the son of a shopkeeper or small farmer; a daily communicant who saw nothing much wrong with Ireland that shooting a few policemen couldn't put right.

An insight into the mentality of the IRA was provided by a recent interview with a member of the 'Old' IRA (that is, one who served in the period 1919-1921), shown in Robert Kee's *Ireland – A Television History*. The by now very elderly gentleman, sixty-odd years ago one of Michael Collins's so-called 'Death Squad', told Mr Kee with evident pleasure of how he and some of his comrades received communion before going to carry out a killing. He described his own confession before the communion thus: 'I told him a few small sins first and kept the big one to last', after which he received not only absolution, but also a blessing for following his conscience. The 'big one' was presumably his intention to kill somebody, and therefore the blessing was, one imagines, for intending to do it in accordance with the dictates of his conscience. It is always nice to see priest and penitent in such harmonious agreement.

The Spanish Civil War of 1936-39 put a strain on this simple faith, however. Ireland's home-grown fascists, the Blue Shirts, backed Franco, so the IRA, of necessity, was obliged to support the Spanish Republicans, and with them all the forces of the Left. For some IRA men this was easy and natural, but for others it was a dilemma. For still others it was the Road to Damascus.

The Second World War complicated matters still further. Germany was England's enemy and therefore Ireland's friend – but Germany was fascist, like Franco, and therefore the IRA's enemy. Or was it? Some IRA leaders failed to work out this problem all through the war, and worked for Germany while denouncing Franco. They also denounced de Valera as England's lackey, and some of them got shot for their pains, de Valera feeling that this would teach them *real-politik*. The IRA story was that de Valera had been an English secret agent since 1916, and was one still. That the English secret service had arranged his escape from his Welsh prison camp after the Easter Rising, and had financed his career ever since. (Which reminds one of the frequent Russian discoveries that long-serving Communist leaders have all the time been working for America.)

After the war, and the bombing campaign in which Brendan Behan got himself sent to borstal, the IRA fell into a decline. Few in numbers, weak in influence, without prestige, it existed as a shadow, like a ninety-year-old Grand Duchess in exile whom everyone believes to be long dead. In the sixties, the leadership began a period of self-analysis, and came up with revolutionary answers: Socialism was in; terrorism – *vide* Lenin – was out. The way forward lay in influencing and educating the masses.

Around 1967 the IRA's leadership presented its remaining Second World War armoury – about half-a-dozen not-very-serviceable revolvers, by most accounts – to the Welsh Liberation Army, and set about exploiting working-class discontent in the North. This discontent was mainly Catholic, but not exclusively so. Even more than the South, the North had remained fixed in the soft glue of time – around 1910. Great Protestant landowners and industrialists ruled unchallenged. If their Protestant workers grumbled about anything there were hints that the real cause of the trouble was the Catholic minority, unemployed, unemployable, breeding like cockroaches, ready at the drop of a priest's collar to cut any Protestant throat in reach. While if the Catholics complained about anything they were taken aside and given a good hammering by the Royal Ulster Constabulary. And Catholics in the North had a lot to grumble about. They were discriminated against in jobs, in housing, in welfare and above all in political representation, constituencies for both parliament and local councils being so arranged that no Catholic could achieve office, even where the number of potential Catholic voters ought to have made success certain. The system, invented in America, and widely copied elsewhere, was known as gerrymandering (Mr Eldbridge Gerry was a Harvard man, class of 1762. As Governor of Massachusetts, 1810-12, he invented the system in order to preserve the state for the Republican interests – the resultant map of the new distribution resembled a salamander, until someone remarked that it should be called a 'Gerry-mander'. One might have supposed him to be of Irish descent, but his family came from Devonshire.)

The IRA's intention was to exploit both Catholic and Protestant working-class distress and discontent, educate both to the point where they realised that their common social and political interests far outweighed their religious differences, and, having forged the Ulster masses into a revolutionary political weapon, sweep away Stormont and set up a Socialist government in its place. That achieved, they could then turn their eyes south to where their real ambitions lay, and create a Marxist Irish Republic, a new Cuba, not by military invasion, although at some stage insurrection would not be absolutely excluded, but by applying all the pressure of civil disbodience and political violence that a united and well-led working-class can exert.

It was an ambitious project, but in 1968-69 it looked as if it was getting under way. The Civil Rights Movement, by no means an IRA invention, was nevertheless falling into IRA control, and was gaining successes. (The object of the Civil Rights protesters was to obtain, by non-violent, Gandhian protests and actions, equality for Catholics in Northern Ireland. Ever since 1919 it had been a bitter cause of resentment in the North that Catholics were actively discriminated against in every sphere of life; in jobs, in housing, in promotion in the Civil Service, in welfare payments, and even in voting. If successive British governments had really considered Northern Ireland to be 'a part of the United Kingdom' they would have put these glaring injustices right, and thus saved a vast amount of bloodshed and destruction over the past fifteen years. The Provisional IRA are not 'simply criminals' – no criminals could obtain the degree of support the Provisionals enjoy in the North. They obtain that support because they are the only people actively attempting to set these injustices right. One may condemn their methods, but at least they are doing *something*. No one else did *anything* between 1919 and 1969.) At which point the real rulers of Ulster inspired Protestant mobs to attack the Catholics. There were ugly pogroms, and a danger of civil war. The Catholics broadcast desperate appeals for help to the Dublin government and to the Southern people, both for arms and allies.

In this crisis the IRA leadership was sharply divided. The new, sixties-style, Marxist leadership was appalled at the prospect of an armed struggle between two fractions of the working-class – a struggle in which both they and the working-class itself were certain to be the chief victims. They – the Marxist leaders – called for patience, political savvy and, if necessary, political martyrdom. Out of evil would come good; out of martyrdom would come power.

But just below the top leadership level there was another element in the IRA, the second-rank leadership, harking back to the days of Catholic Nationalism, and deeply distrustful of Marxism, Socialism and all the working-class jargon that went with them. They accused the leadership of cowardice, and worse, of treachery. Why had the IRA's arms been given to the Welsh? To the bloody Welsh! And now! Look! Protestants on the rampage and not a bullet to put between their ugly eyes. Damn all the sophisticated talk – let's kill some Prods.

Into this quarrel there entered agents of the Southern government. Ostensibly they came to ask what, within the bounds possible for a government, could be done to help the Catholics? Money for the Red Cross? Food? Shelter in the South for refugees? Under this respectable camouflage some of the agents asked other questions: Would the IRA's second-rank leadership like to have arms? And money for more arms? And here it needs to be said that, ever since, the fiercest argument has continued in the South as to what exactly *was* said in those negotiations, and who said it, and by who's authority. The official version is that if these things *were* said, it was not on government authority. Various Southern government ministers were accused of acting without government authority, on their own Republican initiative. Eventually they were tried in court for alleged offences of arms smuggling arising from these talks, and all were acquitted. But none of the central questions were satisfactorily answered, in court or elsewhere. £100,000 of Dublin government money, supposedly voted for Red Cross relief, was never accounted for from that day to this, and the question of how much, if anything, the then Taoiseach, Mr Jack Lynch, knew about what was or was not going on has never been answered and presumably never will be.

But, keeping the laws of libel firmly in mind, what seems to have happened is this. *Some* agent, acting on the authority of *some* element in the Dublin establishment, offered the second-rank, non-Marxist leadership of the IRA a bargain: 'Ditch your Marxist leaders. Renounce Marxism and all ambitions to overturn the Southern government, and we'll arm and finance you.'

The bargain was accepted and the 'Provisional' IRA was born, hiving off from the Marxist-led Official IRA. In the succeeding years the Officials have faded into the background and have several times been pronounced dead and buried. The Provisionals, the 'Provos', have gone from strength to fearful strength. Internment was their greatest advantage. The H-Blocks, the Hunger Strikes – far be it from me to suggest what could have been done instead, but every step taken, by Stormont first and London since, seems designed to strengthen the hold of the Provos on Catholic imaginations. Whenever there seems a faint possibility that that hold might slacken and fail, the English authorities – all right, British – perform some other macabre act of self-defeat: Bloody Sunday; the torture of detainees (many of them truly and genuinely unconnected with any relevant event), the *defence* of torture, and the denial that it was or *is* torture; the use of plastic bullets ('unthinkable' for use in England, as Mr Whitelaw rightly said); the failure to make any attempt to understand *why* the Provos can continue to represent Catholics, or to understand in any degree what the Catholic grievances were and are; the failure to denounce past injustices or promise effective future remedies; the failure to control Protestant ruffianism or to regard it *as* ruffianism; the collapse in the face of Protestant threats of a general strike; the failure to defuse the Hunger Strike and H-Block situations before they caused more useless deaths and misery. Any decent Irishman must be ashamed that murderers can claim to represent him, or rather, Ireland. But any decent Englishman *should* be ashamed that his government has been so monumentally futile over so long a period. Thirteen years at the time of writing these lines. How many more years? How many more deaths? Ruined lives? Ruined buildings?

And since for the moment I am addressing an imaginary English audience – what should you English have done? One of two things. You should, ten or more years ago, have been ruthless, instead of half ruthless. A surgeon cannot cut off a patient's leg slowly. You should have told your army to solve the problem, no matter who was killed or how it was done, and then have incorporated the North firmly and for ever into the United Kingdom. You keep saying it's like Yorkshire. Then treat it like Yorkshire. Equal votes for all. Equal laws, with Mr Paisley as firmly subject to them as Paddy O'Gormless.

Or, if you lacked the stomach for all of that, then you should have gone and left the Irish to solve an Irish problem. But, you say, it would have caused a blood-bath. There has *been* a blood-bath. Thirteen years of blood, and many years before that, too. What the Devil are you doing there?

I was born in England, but I live in Ireland. And when I go to Belfast and see English soldiers patrolling the streets in combat fatigue, rifles at the ready, my blood pressure rises in fury. Why the Hell should they be there? By what right? By what right is part of Ireland claimed to be 'part of the United Kingdom'? Conquest, that's all.And if my placid blood threatens to boil, what is it like for genuine Irish men and women?

Would *you* like to see London streets patrolled by Belgian soldiers? Or French? Or American (because the UK is 'part of NATO')? Have your car stopped and searched by them? You might like the soldiers very much, as human beings, but you would not want them in London. In control. We don't want you in Belfast. In control. Go away. Leave us alone. If we then kill each other, it's our affair, not yours. Who gave you the right to call it your affair? When? For nearly fifty years you were content to have nothing to do with Ulster, when again and again you could have helped, could have insisted on justice for the minority. Why become so interested now?

And why are you so sure that Ulster cannot cope with Ulster's problems, and Ireland with Ireland's? You were sure that the 'gyppoes' could not run the Suez Canal – they've run it better than you did. You were certain that India could never survive its independence – it has. And Cyprus. And Kenya. And Uncle Tom Cobley. Why not us? Go away, go away, go away. And then, when the dust has settled, and the blood dried, we can be true friends. Then too we can recognise that we really are absolutely the same, that there really is no difference between Irish and English that matters a damn.

After which burst of unaccustomed and ill-judged passion, allow me please to return to the proper subject of this book, if it has a proper subject, which is to look at Ireland, and in so far as one man can hope to draw a portrait – or anyway a rough, lightning sketch – of his country, to draw one, and in doing so perhaps to strike on differences, or characteristics, or traits that will explain to you why we are as we are. Or if not why – and really I have already offered as much of a why as I ever expect to hit on – then how, and in what small ways we differ from you who are not Irish. I know in advance, of course, that such an attempt is futile, and foredoomed not only to failure, but to the most bitter criticism from all sides of Irish society – in the unlikely event of 'Irish society' becoming aware of this book. I have therefore thought to spare the critics too much labour by including some at least of their likely criticisms in the book itself, a labour-saving device that ought to become widespread. And in order to do this I have allowed an imaginary, but not too imaginary, 'Establishment Spokesperson' to enter the argument. As cultured as I am uncouth, she will at intervals represent all that is truly Irish in contrast to my own un-Irish contributions – you may, if you like, in the Irish Civil Service to ensure that the real values of Ireland the Irish Civil Service to ensure that the real values of Ireland counter the foreign misconceptions in the world's headlines.

3 A Classless Society

We Irish like to think that we can see through pretentiousness and snobbery, and fondly boast that ours is as nearly as possible a classless society. We tell each other that we value a friend, or anyone, for what he or she is, and not for what they possess. We enjoy it very much when the rich and pompous slip on a banana skin, and we like it even more when the British do so, because they are our rich relations. But there is no malice in this, or anyway not very much, and what there is is human rather than Irish.

But this boast of ours being a classless society needs more examination before it can be accepted. Certainly Southern Ireland has no officially recognised aristocracy, since the Constitution forbids our government to grant honours to citizens for fear of creating any sort of élite. Yet to pretend that Ireland is democratically and republicanly classless is absolute nonsense. Our class system is as extensive and subtle as its British counterpart, if not more so, with the one difference that it does not lead gently upwards to one Everest peak of unquestioned honour and social authority in the person of a monarch, but rather to a series of unrelated peaks, as if in Ireland there was not one class system recognised by everyone, but half a dozen.

We have a President, of course, and everyone regards him as the Head of State, but this is a long way from granting him unquestioned social prestige. I have never met anyone who went into contortions attempting to get invited to a Presidential garden party – indeed, I have never even heard that Presidential garden parties exist. I have never heard anyone whispering in awed reverence that so-and-so was the President's second cousin on the wife's side. Irish women's magazines show almost no interest in the inner life of the Presidential family – the whole family is non-existent as far as the average Irish man or woman is concerned. All that sort of gasping interest is reserved for the British Royal Family. We would adore to know what Queen Elizabeth eats for breakfast, but whether our President spreads marmalade on his sausages we neither know nor care.

In fact, the whole prestige of the office took a terrible knock a few years ago when a government minister stated publicly and with bluff irascibility that the President of the day was a thundering disgrace. The President made signals to the Prime Minister of the day, calling for something appropriate to be done about this, and then, feeling that he was receiving a lot less than the essential minimum of governmental support, resigned. The effect was rather as if the British Home Secretary had said at a banquet that the Queen was a dirty trollop, and that she had then abdicated.

For a few moments a great volume of public sympathy was generated for the unhappy President, and a vast amount of breath was wasted gossiping about exactly why it had all been allowed to happen. But within a brief period the sympathy subsided to more modest proportions, and people began to tell each other that if it had been Dev in the case (Mr de Valera, the chief, the unquestionably great man of modern Ireland), then by the Holy it wouldn't have happened like that at all. Whether Dev had been Taoiseach or President – he was Prime Minister for many years and then President for many more – whichever he had been when such a scandal attempted to erupt, it wouldn't have got to the starting gate.

If any of Dev's ministers ever had ideas of speaking out of turn, one icy glance from him and they forgot them, as if they had been struck by lightning. And if, when Dev had retired from the active slaughter of Irish politics and was living in the Presidential lodge, a brash young faggot of a new minister had dreamed of saying that Dev was anything less than the Angel Gabriel, his skin would have been had for trousers. Dev was a man. He was more than a man. He was a politician. He was more than a politician. He was an *Irish* politician. Where are the snows of yesteryear?

Ever since Dev's translation to the Elysian Fields, the prestige of the Presidency has been in gentle decline, and the 'thundering disgrace' incident (given a peculiarly Irish dimension because the speech that contained the phrase was delivered to a gathering of senior army officers, not one of whom was reported as having protested) delivered a very hard knock to what then remained. Our President is a charming man. All our Presidents are charming men. But they are retired politicians, put forward by one of the political parties after obscure and not always savoury political manoeuvres, and elected in campaigns as ferocious as they are meaningless – meaningless because we are electing someone who has no effective power. We are not electing an American president, whose future actions will have great importance. We are electing the equivalent of a constitutional monarch, whose only value to us is, or ought to be, the near universal respect in which he or she is regarded. And in the process of electing a President we do almost everything possible to diminish that essential respect.

It's an Irish solution to an Irish problem, and our President is reduced to a kindly man who receives foreign ambassadors. (He is always pictured knee to knee with them in the presidential drawing room, smiling ecstatically as if he had just been told a tremendous joke in basic Chinese and had failed to get the point.)

The President, therefore, is not regarded in Ireland as the unquestioned head of society, except in official handouts. Who is? Well, no one. And several people, depending on your prejudices. If you are an ardent Fianna Fáil supporter, then the head of Irish society, unquestioned, due all the reverence and moist-eyed love of any high king of old, is the Leader of the Party. (Who according to you has a Divine right also to be Leader of the Country. During those appalling interregnums when 'the Other Crowd' are in, crops fail, there are snowstorms in July, cows give birth to two-headed calves, the fishing is a disaster. But God usually intervenes before too long, and things are put right again at the next General Election.)

However, even this basic certainty of Irish life is no longer rock solid. Some of the petty kings of the Grand Old Party have their little battle-axes out and swinging in an effort to shorten the high king. This is mainly over events of twelve or more years ago, connected with the Northern Troubles and who did or didn't do what about providing arms for the beleaguered Catholics, but it has other factors, ranging from sheer personal hatreds to charges of ineffectiveness – when the high king is impotent the crops fail just as surely as when 'the Other Crowd' gets in. These ructions will not come to an end until someone's head is lopped and attached to the victor's belt. (A not-much-publicised practice in ancient Ireland was head-hunting. Heroes regularly carried around their victims' heads to produce triumphantly at the next warriors' feast, which must have made entertaining an alarming business.)

Compared to the jolly brutality and extroversion of Fianna Fáil, the other crowd, Fine Gael, are a demure, self-analysing lot, beset by intellectualism and self-doubt. Their leaders live in the posh Dublin suburbs like Foxrock and Donnybrook, rather than on the honest, simple 500-acre estates of the 'the Real Party', or the good strong cattle ranches of the midlands where the Heart of Ireland still beats loud and true.

Fine Gaelers are descended from the crowd that accepted Partition and the Treaty, and that ran the Free State for the first ten years of its existence. They fought and won the Civil War of 1921-23 against die-hard Republicans led by de Valera (who didn't accept the Treaty or Partition or the oath of allegiance or anything else, until he suddenly discovered that these things were only a form of words and not worth fighting about. Whereupon he fought a general election, won it, became Taoiseach, and started putting his old friends in gaol if they uttered a cheep of protest. He was like Henry IV of France finding Paris to be 'well worth a Mass'. He was a real politician. In his time the crops never failed.)

But these Fine Gaelers, 'the Other Crowd' – in the beginning, in the twenties, they tended to be Protestant-oriented, West British-oriented, big business-oriented, eager to reassure 'the old crowd' (the British, the Ascendancy, Big Capital, and so on) that although they were, most of them, Catholics and sort-of-kind-of Nationalists, they were *sensible* nationalists, *rational* nationalists, not Republicans, not *extremists*. To prove this, they shot lots of Republicans during the Civil War, a fact which the Republicans, the Real party, have never forgotten to this day.

During the sixties the Fine Gaelers tried to get rid of their conservative, un-Republican, stick-in-the-mud image by dreaming up a blueprint for a New Society which would Appeal To The Young. Younger tabby cats were brought forward and dressed up as young tigers, and everything was going to change, to change utterly. But the Fine Gael Old Guard, which still yearned for the simplicities of the twenties and thirties, when what counted was to be a daily communicant, soon put a stop to the nonsense.

At a moment in 1974 when Fine Gael was in power and a Great Moral issue was to be voted on – with the young tigers pressing for liberalism – the leader of Fine Gael suddenly got up to vote against his own party and his own party's proposal. Fortunately 'the Real Crowd' got in soon afterwards and things got back to normal. But it left its effects on the members of Fine Gael, who have never really recovered their poise. Everyone knows that the leader of Fine Gael is a *nice* man and an *honest* man and a *good* man. But is he a chief? Would he see to the crops? And the answer has to be 'No'. He wouldn't even know a crop of barley from a field of wheat. He keeps on *talking*. And spouting statistics. And having theories. He is not a Chief.(Since writing these optimistic lines, disaster has struck. There has been an election and 'the Other Crowd' has got in, helped by 'the Small Crowd', laughingly known as the Irish Labour Party. The weather has got worse already.)

All of which has distracted us a little from Irish society. But not much, because although the leader of Fine Gael is not a chief, he has social prestige. So have his nearest and dearest followers, 'the Donnybrook Set'. Professors. Economists. Political Analysts. Theorists. Lord love a duck, man, it isn't theories you need to run a country, it's votes, a simple fact of political life which even yet has not penetrated Fine Gael. And in Irish life politics and society are so closely allied, so overlapping as to be hard to separate one from the other. But perhaps they are in England, and elsewhere, too?

Anyway, that's one social hierarchy in the Irish social mountain range. Another is the horsey lot. The horse was a sacred animal in ancient Ireland, and it still is. (Brendan Behan described the Ascendancy* as a Protestant on a horse.) The Mecca of the horse

* The Protestant Ascendancy was the ruling class of Ireland in the 18th century when for periods Ireland possessed her own parliament. Only Protestants could sit, and members were drawn from or were protégés of the Protestant landowning

hierarchy is the Royal Dublin Society and the Horse Show, where men in bowler hats and tweed suits walk about carrying shooting-sticks, and their wives eat strawberries and ask each other what happened to darling Lucinda whom they haven't seen for ages. They go to Hunt Balls, and entertain each other, and are mostly Protestant and West British (meaning that they went to school in England and talk about the Queen instead of the Queen of England. So, for that matter, do we, but they speak as if they know her personally, as perhaps they do.)

These horse families mostly live in Georgian mansions in Tipperary or County Meath. They are almost all descended from English settlers, and some of them have titles. They regard the surrounding sea of Catholics with deep suspicion, and thus are convinced that no one would allow them to take part in Irish public life. They never stand for the Dáil, or their local councils. They *expect* to be discriminated against. They never learn Irish (neither do we, properly, but the horse people don't even *pretend*), and they call Gaelic 'Gallic', or 'Erse', if they want to be rude.* When not wearing bowlers the men wear little trilby hats a size too small and tipped forward over their eyebrows; the girls learn Cordon Bleu cooking as a Preparation for Life, and poison their boyfriends with Oeufs à la Crème de Menthe.

Although they never entertain Catholics in their houses (except an occasional tame one, such as a local doctor who happens to strike their fancy), the horse people do have Catholic friends – racehorse trainers, for example, and the kind of cattle-dealer who goes shooting. At the peak of this particular hierarchy there are earls and even a duke or so, and at the bottom of it rich Americans – preferably from the Old South – who have bought Irish estates and done them up and entered into the swing of things. They all seem to drive Range Rovers or Land Rovers or estate cars towing horse-boxes, and to have very loud voices, as if used to talking to the

gentry. The term Ascendancy outlived its technical usage and came to mean the Protestant gentry in general. Of course there were poor Protestants too.

* Gaelic is the Celtic language of Ireland and Scotland and the Isle of Man, differing very considerably from the Brythonic Celtic of Wales and Cornwall and Brittany. Erse is a name sometimes used for Irish Gaelic, which (for reasons of sound perhaps?) struck some non-Gaelic speakers as tremendously humorous.

deaf or the dull of mind. To the best of their great social abilities they keep alive the traditions of England in 1910.

Why they don't enter into the generality of Irish life is a mystery. **No one dislikes** them as individuals. Almost everyone is prepared to like them, and two Presidents in our short sequence have been Protestants. Most Irish people are mad about some aspect of the horse world, even if it's only buying a ticket in the Irish Hospital Sweepstakes, so if some of the Anglo-Irish got into the Daíl it could prove to be very valuable for all concerned.

The difficulty is that no matter how much these Anglo-Irish might disclaim the description, they are colonials, as much so as if they were living in Hong Kong or Kenya. For them, everything Irish is irredeemably second-best, whether it is the government or the plumbing. Good things come from England, from Fortnums, or Harrods, or Boots, or Savile Row. The real government is in Westminster, not in Dublin; the only real education is an English one; the only worthwhile service is that devoted to the remains of the British Empire. Just to live in Ireland, even after five hundred years of Irish residence, is second-best. The really great houses are in England; the really great families are English; the only titles of nobility that possess real prestige are English titles – even an Irish dukedom has something faintly raffish, second-class about it. A really fine marriage for the daughter of even a great Anglo-Irish family would leave her in possession of an English stately home, with a husband in the House of Lords.

And all this even though the stately home may have become an amusement park for tourists, and the English nobility may sigh for the primeval simplicities of Irish life, where trade unions have not yet become a daily threat to daily comforts. The Anglo-Irish may shudder at modern England as a taxi brings them through the horrors of Soho, or they may see and regret the degradation of famous shops reduced to selling things from Korea and sending out bills after only a month or so. But their hearts have not yet accepted these changes as reality. In their dreams England is still what it was before 1914, or at least before 1939, the centre of the Universe, the *beau idéal* of gracious living and imperial virtue, and all that has happened since is a nightmare that must surely vanish with the dawn, of which, perhaps, Mrs Thatcher is the herald, the slightly odd

Aurora. Meanwhile, they live in Ireland, but not as part of it.

Yet although this retreat, this disdainful, defensive aloofness from the mainstream of Irish life, is the hallmark of the horse society, it would be unjust as well as unkind to leave that as the last word on it. Many of the Anglo-Irish have other qualities besides that of being anachronisms. Some of them have gained true distinction in the British service. Some are patrons of the arts. Those who have money use it, in the main, for the benefit of their neighbourhood. Those who have not would be the last people in Ireland to expect the State to look after them. Some, whether rich or poor, are wise and good, some are bad and interesting, nearly all are charming, in the old-fashioned sense of the word. They exercise charm as a part of their natural way of life and they have, with a few exceptions, excellent manners at a time when even passable manners are becoming something to remark upon. And they live in a way that most of us could imitate with profit, whether in such small affairs as changing for dinner, or in such larger ones as regarding their estates as sources of beauty rather than of profit only, and as a heritage for the future.

What we have in Ireland of man-made beauty we owe to their ancestors, who built our fine houses, and laid out our fine gardens and avenues of noble trees. What is still preserved of these things we owe to the fathers of our present-day horse people. Such little as our town clerks and county councillors and gombeen men will allow to survive into a future generation we will owe very largely to those men in bowler hats and those women in tweeds and twin-sets whom we affect to laugh at because so often we envy them. I repeat, that it is a sin, and a loss to Ireland, that they take so little part in public affairs here.

But just as Fine Gaelers and Fianna Fáilers can't forget what happened during the Civil War, the horse people can't forget what happened during the Troubles that preceded the Civil War, when an alarming number of their stately homes were burned to the ground – often never to be rebuilt. Although, to be fair, extremely few of the horse people were actually shot during the Troubles, and ever since successive Irish governments have shown themselves to be admirably tolerant of living relics of the past. (Dead relics, such as Nelson's Pillar in Dublin and various other military and naval monuments to British imperial greatness, have had shorter shrift, although not necessarily from governments. It is, incidentally, supposed that Breton Nationalists were imported to blow up the Pillar. They laid it the length of O'Connell Street with wonderful precision, and didn't kill a living soul in the process. Of course, no one ever discovered who actually arranged the destruction.)

Turning aside from the horse people, there is the Jet Set, the Café Society and the Artistic Aristocracy – a complex social hierarchy headed by the Guinness family. (Why selling beer should produce so much social prestige and glamour is another mystery, but one shared with England, where beer barons also abound. Though so do whisky earls, such as Earl Haig. In Germany there is even a lager prince, *hochwohlgeboren*, and reaching the places where other aristocrats never penetrate.)

There is also the hierarchy of the rich – the commercially rich – whose status depends merely on their possessing a great deal of money rather than on the way in which the money was made, or the length of time it has been possessed. But such hierarchies exist in every country. There is nothing peculiarly Irish about them, and, as their peers do elsewhere, the Irish rich possess so much charm and so many graces that to describe them would be to gild refined gold. One can only pass on with reverent step and hushed voice to the remaining hierarchy, if such it can be called, because by now it is only a vestige, an archaeological remnant of what it once was, the old Gaelic aristocracy, with a few Norman-Gaelic additions such as the Knight of Glin and the heads of the other branches of the Geraldines – the only social hierarchy that could fairly be described as genuinely Irish and genuinely aristocratic.

For the real Gaelic nobility no title was necessary. The word 'the' before the chief's name was – and is – enough. The O'Connor Don. The O'Mahony. The O'Kelly. The O'Neill. (Only recently the O'Neill clan had the joy of installing a new chief. He turned out to be Portuguese.) The great moving spirit in reawakening interest in this vestigial Gaelic aristocracy was, in the 1940s to '60s, a man named Eoin O'Mahony – sometimes called 'the Pope O'Mahony', because of his general air of Catholic authority.

He was immensely fat – which made him look rather strange in his uniform as a Knight of Malta, like a black football wearing a sword – and almost penniless. He travelled Ireland, often on foot and carrying a sponge-bag for luggage, looking for places to stay. *Great* places, for he was not much interested in the proletariat. And when he did find a noble house to welcome him – as he always did, for he was much loved – he rewarded his hosts with an endless stream of information about Irish genealogies, and particularly those relevant to his hosts. He knew the details of every noble birth and death and marriage and misdemeanour that ever took place in Ireland, and in many countries besides. Merely to mention an obscure noble name would be to set him off on a lecture lasting several hours and ranging from the high kings of Tara to the O'Donnells of Donegal to the O'Sullivans of Cork and Kerry to who courted whose sister in 1931 and jilted her for a Chicago heiress. He was a living *Almanach de Gael*.

Finally – I may have left out a hierarchy or two but it doesn't matter – there is the minor hierarchy of 'personalities', as there is in every country. The fashionable poet, the fashionable portrait painter, the sought-after fashion designer, the best-selling author, the TV presenter. These claimants to social notice are ephemeral, and yesterday's 'famous personality' is often today's '*Who* did you say?'

One of the few exceptions to this ephemerality is the presenter of *The Late Late Show*, Gay Byrne, whose TV programme has been a significant feature of Irish life for twenty-one years. More than any politician or professional 'social reformer', he has widened Irish horizons, to the point where it is now possible to discuss such things as sex in public, without being excommunicated, or driven into exile. The fact that Ireland in the 1980s has a different mental climate to that of the 1950s owes an enormous amount to Mr Byrne and his courage in allowing controversial matters to be discussed on his chat show.

This has not always brought him undiluted praise. His most recent run in with the unco' guid erupted over his invitation to 'Madame Sin', the notorious English brothel-keeper, to appear on his show and defend her activities. On the same show an English woman journalist admitted to having had an abortion.

The backwoods of Ireland blew up. The economy might be in ruins. The North might be in bloody ruins. What obsessed the pressure groups was Madame Sin and the woman journalist's abortion. The Chairman of the television authority apologised to all and sundry. The Director-General apologised to all and sundry. Gay Byrne, teeth gritted, was forced to apologise. A new minister for something-or-other, just appointed by the Wrong Crowd, screeched that all this carry-on would be put a stop to, so it would.

(At much the same moment as 'the Awful Programme' was being transmitted, a poor, half-demented girl flung her five-month-old baby into a canal, in despair at finding anywhere to live, or any means of feeding it. By chance a boy noticed it floating on the surface and rescued it. The baby survived. The girl was caught, presumably to go to gaol eventually, to teach her not to become a mother again, at least not until she had a private income. In fact the court, with great humanity, put her on probation and sent her home to be cared for by whoever had failed to care for her before, and had allowed her to reach that state of despair.

Every night of the week, teenage prostitutes, some only thirteen years old, parade beside the canal bridges in bum-freezer mini-skirts, soliciting customers. But neither those unfortunates nor the unmarried mothers of whom the aforementioned mother was an extreme example, arouse much interest in the breasts of Irish moralists. No minister, new or old, of any crowd, has ever announced that a stop should be put to such carryings-on. That sort of wrath is reserved for more important matters, such as TV programmes. Yet here again, is Irish hypocrisy so different from the English variety? Are our unco' guid any more unco' guid than yours? Mrs Mary Whitehouse would find herself instantly at home in Dublin.)

And post-finally, again as in all other countries, there are the people with no social prestige to speak of at all, but who really run the country and give it the value it has. The judges, and the professors, and newspaper editors, and top civil servants, and headmasters and headmistresses and people who sit on unpaid committees and senior Garda officers and army officers and the clergy and businessmen and professional men and the ones I've forgotten to mention, exactly as there are in England and France and America and the Seychelle Islands.

(ESTABLISHMENT SPOKESPERSON: I've been listening to all of that and I don't like any of it. You're making a jeer of us again. What have the Seychelle Islands got to do with anything? Where are they, anyway?

CLEEVE: I'm not making a jeer. I'm being deeply respectful. I didn't even make that joke about 'the cream of society' [thick and rich].

ES: And well you might not. What do you know about society, good, bad or indifferent? Did anyone even ask you out to dinner this ten years past? Were you ever asked to meet the President? Would any of the Guinnesses even give you the time of day if they ran you over in their Rolls-Royce?

C: I once saw de Valera as close as I am to you now. He nearly trod on my toe.

ES: A pity he didn't. You're green with jealousy, that's all. 'The horse people', forsooth. Don't you know that the bloodstock industry is one of Ireland's greatest assets? That Irish horses are exported all over the world? That they win all before them wherever they go? That –

C: I know! I know! I didn't say a word against them.

ES: – that the National Stud is one of the chief wonders and envies of the sporting world? That maharajahs keep their horses here because the training is the best in the world and the grass is the best in the world and the grooms are the best in the world and the tax relief is the best in the world and –

C: I know. I know. It was just a-sort-of-a-kind-of-a joke. No offence in the world intended. And didn't I say the President is a nice man? And that Garrett is a nice man? And a *good* man? And an *honest* man? Didn't I say that? Did I even mention Shergar?

ES: You said it all with that class of a jeer you put on everything. I'll tell you for nothing, people won't like it. The Plain People of Ireland don't like sarcasm, or jeers, or bad jokes about Important People. The Plain People have Respect. They like Decency. They know their place. Didn't a Grand Duke and a Grand Duchess come here only the other day and didn't everyone cheer them and say how handsome they looked? Not a jeer, not a dirty word of sarcasm. Just Respect. Decency. And the President –

C: Wasn't that the time all the guards were out on their motorcycles clearing the traffic and a man wrote in to the papers and said that if only a couple of the guards had been down at the North Wall the same day his daughter wouldn't have got her car knocked open and her handbag stolen and her nerves in tatters for a week after?

ES: I'm going to report this. I'm not going to stand any more of it.

Do you not know that the Garda Siochana are the finest body of men to be found in the length and breadth and four corners of the world? That their chief glory is that from the very beginning they've refused to carry arms, even when the Civil War was still raging?

C: I know. I know. But did you hear that in the old days, the Free State days, a lot of civil servants used to keep revolvers in their in-trays in case they got unwelcome visitors? You know – someone from the Real Crowd wanting an argument. And talking about the civil service, do you remember about the Russian 'Crown Jewels' that some of the lads in New York bought off the Bolshevik delegation in 1919 or thereabouts? For £20,000 no less, the Russians being in need of money to pay their hotel bill, and our lads being well got with Irish Americans pressing donations on them? Well, those jewels –

ES: I don't want to hear this.

C: Well, those Crown Jewels were knocking about in a drawer in an office up in the Phoenix Park for years and years. They turned out to be a load of costume jewellery.

ES: You're lying again. All this is dirty propaganda. You should be ashamed.

C: And do you remember the *Irish* Crown Jewels, the regalia lot? The Knights of St Patrick collars and the other things? How they were all stolen one night just before King Edward arrived? He was livid. I heard the Pope O'Mahony say once he knew where they were to that day, hidden in the roof of a house in Clyde Road. They were offered back to the government – *our* government, not the British of course – for £5,000, but we wouldn't pay. And so they're still there. Will I tell them about that?

ES: You will not tell them! I forbid it!

C: They'd like to hear. The Viceroy of the day was a queer fish to begin with. At the viceregal garden parties he used to give the visitors currant buns. He said he couldn't afford anything else. And his wife had pawned her ear-rings and got the diamonds replaced with paste. They were family heirlooms and there was a terrible row about it when the family found out.

ES: I forbid this, absolutely. I'm going to call the guards. It has nothing to do with –

C: It has so. This *is* society. It's society gossip. It's even true. Well, one night at a bachelor party in the Castle some of the younger set stripped one of the Heralds stark naked (they had got him absolutely pie-eyed on sherry first), and got the key of the safe where the regalia was kept, out of his trousers pocket, and dressed him from head to foot in the collars of the Knights of St Patrick. It was a merry jest. Only next day all the collars and the rest of the regalia were missing. And no one has seen sight nor sign of them to this day, except whoever stole them. There was some nasty talk about it all, I promise you.

ES: This is supposed to be about modern Ireland. Is there no hope of you sticking to the point?

C: But this *is* the point. These are the things that make Ireland what it is. Fey, charming, a delight to tourists, an example to the world. Laetitia Pilkington –

ES: I've heard enough. Will you stop this instant?

C: I was only trying –

ES: This instant.

C: I only wanted –

ES: NOW!)

4 The Church

An Irish bishop said of his flock that its members all held three diametrically opposed and irreconcilable attitudes to death and the other world and religion in general, and held them firmly and all at the same time: that when you were dead, you were dead, and that was that; that what the bishop and Church taught them was true; and that the dead were down there under the ground, plotting against us.

I am certain that this is true of a great many Irish Catholics, although they would not be likely to put it as cynically and succinctly as the bishop. I am not, however, so certain that it is a purely Irish phenomenon. Most people are capable of holding irreconcilable views on many things without ever managing to notice the irreconcilability. Few of us are logical, and I doubt if the average Englishman, or American, or Sudanese, is any more logical than the Irish, either by nature or training.

But it remains that Irish attitudes to religion are illogical. For example, Irish Catholics are immensely fond of resigning themselves to God's will. 'Ah sure, God's will be done. His ways are not our ways. It was His will that –' whatever catastrophe has just struck should have struck. A really old-fashioned Irish Catholic sounds rather like a Moslem in his or her – more usually her – total submission to the will of God. But the same old-fashioned Catholic will be utterly convinced that that same will of God is like putty in her hands.

'Sure don't I always pray to St Jude for what I want, and doesn't he always get it for me?'

'I don't like bothering Our Lady for things too often, She does have enough to be doing as it is. But I've a great faith in St Anne, Her blessed mother –' or in St Joseph, Her blessed husband, or in St Anthony (for finding things), or in St Agnes, or the Little Flower,* or Padre Pio (not yet recognised officially as a saint but surely on the way to canonisation), or any of a hundred other saints who appear to be imagined as messengers constantly on the run between Irish churches and the Throne of God.

As a convert to Catholicism – and converted in England and America, what's worse – I find myself in a continual state of bewilderment at Irish Catholic beliefs and practices. I find myself wondering again and again, is this the same religion that I myself imagine I belong to? In my foreign-bred arrogance as a convert, I see Irish Catholic belief as a collection of pagan superstitions, loosely held together by the Apostles' Creed.

In this Irish Catholics are no different from Spanish or Italian or South American or African Catholics, and for all I know from Japanese or Austrian Catholics – except that the Irish make such a furore about *being* Catholics, rather like one of those maiden aunts who feels the whole family would fall to bits if she wasn't there to keep things on the right road.

Ireland has indeed done more than its fair share in spreading the Gospel, but an unkind observer is left wondering exactly what kind of Gospel it is that the Irish are spreading. Of course, Father O'Toole the missionary in Bolivia, and Bishop O'Grundy, and Father O'Sullivan the theologian, are not likely to hold exactly the same simple views as Mrs Murphy of Ballymagash.

Yet Mrs Murphy exists, and in large numbers, and it is indeed true that the Church fails to make any attempt to correct her view that the Heavenly Hierarchy is there to solve her personal problems, and will do so in return for spiritual bribes. But, as I've just suggested,

* The Little Flower is the name given to St Thérèse of Lisieux, 1873-97, a Carmelite nun canonised in 1925, and object of deep devotion among Catholics. Padre Pio, a Franciscan, was a famous stigmatic – carrying the bleeding marks of Christ's wounds in his hands and feet and side. He died on 23 September 1968 and is currently being put forward as a candidate for canonisation.

Irish Catholicism offers a wide spectrum of belief and practice (as one would expect), from the sophistication of Jesuit theologians and Dominican Doctors of Canon Law, to the pastoral charity of devoted parish clergy, to the loving care for the poor of the members of the Society of St Vincent de Paul, and the Legion of Mary.

The Legion of Mary, for example, is considered by many Irish Catholics not only to be more typical of Irish Catholicism than Mrs Murphy of Ballymagash, but to be one of its greatest glories, and a proof that Ireland in the 20th century is as vitally Christian as it was in the great days of St Columba. Others are less enthusiastic, however, and see in the Legion an unsympathetic Puritanism, and a lack of intellect. Its founder, Frank Duff, a Dublin layman, while expressing those two charges in very different words, would have accepted them, regarding them not at all as charges but as compliments, and descriptions of one part of his intention.

The Legion had its beginnings among young women members of the Society of St Vincent de Paul, and its first objects were to visit the poor women of a local hospital, to do for them whatever was possible of a charitable nature, and also to attempt to convert young Dublin prostitutes. Within ten years this modest beginning had developed into a movement stretching from New Mexico to India and Australia. By the end of the 1940s the Legion had spread to every part of the world open to Catholic charitable and missionary activity, and already one of its lay missionaries, a young woman called Miss Edel Quinn, was regarded as the Legion's first martyr and saint. In the Philippines the local branch of the Legion was cut off from the rest of the movement by the Second World War and the Japanese invasion. After the liberation of the islands, however, that branch was found to have grown tenfold, in spite of the Japanese occupation, or perhaps because of it.

Since then the Legion has been active not only in the non-Communist world – and large parts of the non-Communist world are far from friendly to real Catholic activities – but even in Communist China, where, to the Legion's pride, it has been called Public Enemy No. 1.

An equally fast-spreading movement of devotion in Ireland – although not Irish in origin – is Charismatic Renewal, whose followers believe that often the Holy Spirit speaks audibly through them at meetings, using strange and incomprehensible tongues.

(They seem not to have read St Paul's comments on this phenomenon
– 1 Cor. 14:6-19 – with any great attention, but that is their affair.)

Yet another powerful influence in Irish Catholicism is the Spanish
Society or movement of Opus Dei, whose ideals are impeccably
Christian, but whose public relations are appalling, leaving the firm
conviction in many unkind observers that it is a secret society
interested principally in political and social power, and exercising an
undue influence over many of their young recruits.

Then there are hearty priests who believe in wearing polo-necked
sweaters and playing guitars in pubs – not many of these, Irish
bishops being still a strait-laced lot – and there are practical priests
who run farmers' co-operatives, or football pools for charity, or
Bingo sessions for the parish funds. There are returned missionaries,
both priests and nuns, who believe in liberation theology, a theology
based on the premise that Christianity is meaningless if it does not
pursue social justice.

These same returned or briefly holidaying missionaries look on the
hedonism and spiritual indifference of the majority of Irish Catholics
with angry contempt, comparing them to the agonies of El Salvador
and other stricken countries. There are priests – and one or two
bishops – who spend their efforts raising funds for the Third World's
hungry millions. There are priests who believe that the struggle in
the North calls them to become involved. Not to take up arms,
although one or two have done even that, and been caught and
condemned, but to speak out against what they see as British and
Protestant injustice to a helpless Catholic minority.

Such priests saw the Hunger Strikers of 1981 not as imprisoned
terrorists seeking prisoner-of-war status and propaganda victories,
but as martyrs prepared to follow their Lord to Calvary in the
pursuit of love and justice for their fellow Catholics. (A great many
Southern Irish Catholics saw them in the same light. For the record,
so did I.)

From all this, any observer would have to say that Ireland is an
intensely religious country. There are lots of churches, and lots of
daily Masses in every church, and lots of people at every Mass. There
is an immense amount of *practice*. People go to confession – not quite
as much as they used to, but they still go. They go to Mass. They go
to communion; the queues to receive communion often stretch the
length of the nave in any large city church. They attend novenas and

first Fridays. They join sodalites and fraternities.

Men still enter for the priesthood, and women still become nuns. Not in such numbers as twenty years ago, to be sure, yet the statistics of the Catholic Church in Ireland remain highly impressive. The Catholic population of the thirty-two counties (Ireland South *and* North) are served by just over 6,000 priests (3,797 diocesan clergy and 2,209 priests belonging to religious orders, including missionary priests serving in the Irish headquarters of their order), which works out at a ratio of one priest per 736 Catholics, including babies. This compares with one priest per 7,000 Catholics in Latin America, one per 1,100 for Western Europe generally, and – closest of all to the Irish figure – one per 900 in the United States. If there is safety in numbers, then the Irish Church is safe.

It looks even safer when one turns to other statistical details, such as the numbers of Orders. For men, there are forty-eight, ranging from the Alexian Brothers and Augustinian Fathers to the Vincentians and White Fathers. They include such communities as the Sons of Divine Providence, the Norbertine Fathers, the Consolata Fathers, and the Legionaries of Christ, none of whom I have ever heard of until now, to my shame. Between fathers, brothers and missionary priests, these forty-eight orders occupy 410 community houses throughout the country.

But even this wealth of commitment is dwarfed by the female Orders. There are 103 of these in Ireland, occupying 832 convents. Daughters of the Cross. Sisters of the Company of Mary. Sisters of the Infant Jesus. Poor Sisters of Nazareth. Sisters of the Visitation. Sisters of St Paul de Chartres. Little Sisters of the Poor. As well as the better known Orders, such as the Irish Sisters of Charity with forty-eight addresses in Dublin alone (perhaps I missed one or two). Who, except someone with experience of convent life, can begin to imagine the intensity of devotion and self-sacrifice hidden behind those unfamiliar names and slightly surprising statistics?

To which statistics one may add four archbishops – one of them a cardinal – thirty-four bishops and seven mitred abbots, not to speak of the lay men and women who devote at least some part of their time and a great deal of their energies to one or another of the lay associations, confraternities, or sodalities of the Church: The Third Order of St Francis, The Pioneer Total Abstinence Association, The

Legion of Mary, The Children of Mary, Opus Dei, Charismatic Renewal, The Society of St Vincent de Paul, and all the other pious and charitable societies that, between them, read and support no less than thirty-eight religious periodicals, from *The Furrow* to *The Capuchin Annual*, to *The Catholic Standard*.

And a few years ago this whole mass of statistics was given meaning and reality and enormously innocent pride when the Pope visited Ireland, the first Pope ever to do so. His visit seemed to breathe a new and even more burning faith into Irish Catholicism, inspiring new vocations, rekindling old ones, and in general reawakening a sometimes dormant interest in religion in the breasts of ordinary Irish people. Pope John Paul II became almost an honorary Irishman. People here adore him, and the simpler the people, the greater the adoration. Higher up the educational scale a degree of caution enters into the feeling: 'He's very *conservative*, isn't he? A bit – a bit reactionary wouldn't you think? Of course it's being Polish and having to stand up to the Communists all his life. But still – in this day and age – you'd imagine ... ' Nevertheless, a million people went to hear him in the Phoenix Park, and another million saw him in the flesh between arriving and leaving. Almost every soul in Ireland watched him on TV, for days on end. Everyone agreed – agrees – that he is wonderful. The young people shrieked and stomped and sang when he said 'I love you'. (They also shrieked and stomped and sang when Mick Jagger threw buckets of water over them at the Rolling Stones concert. The two enthusiasms are by no means incompatible, but one renders the other just a fraction suspect as to the depth, not of its sincerity, but of its meaning.)

To repeat, there is all the evidence that statistics can provide that Catholicism is flourishing in Ireland. The Charismatic Renewal Movement is going from strength to strength. There are Rosary Crusades involving thousands of people. Thousands more go on pilgrimage to Lough Derg. And Knock. And Croagh Patrick. And other centres of pilgrimage in Ireland. Tens of thousands go to Lourdes. There are pilgrimages to the Holy Land. There are special trips to Rome and audiences with the Holy Father. There is a thriving trade in Masses for the dead. In Rosaries. In holy pictures. In holy medals.

Almost every shop you go into has a row of plastic boxes

somewhere on the counter, collecting for missionaries and charitable orders, for Dinners for the Poor and St Anthony's Bread, and a dozen other estimable organisations. Thousands of nuns, thousands of priests and brothers are devoting their lives in Ireland to teaching the young, nursing the sick, caring for the old, succouring the poor. Only a born scoundrel could offer a breath of criticism of this wonderful picture of charity, piety and religious devotion. If Mrs Murphy *does* believe that Heaven is rather like an old Gaelic chieftain's court, where you need a friend to catch God's attention and get Him to listen to your petition, what harm in that? Isn't it innocent enough? Isn't she a good woman, who says her Rosary every morning, noon and night? What more do you want of her?

It is no business of mine to demand anything of Mrs Murphy or to criticise her beliefs. But I think it is fair to point out that while her beliefs are very widely held and respected in Ireland, they are not, in reality, *Catholic* beliefs. True Catholicism is a very demanding religion, but Irish Catholicism is not. To say this may seem like another Irish paradox. Irish Catholicism *seems* demanding enough, particularly for women, and most particularly of all for women like poor Mrs Murphy, who might well describe her life as one long martyrdom of childbirth and submission to a highly unsatisfactory husband. A martyrdom only made bearable by the consolations of prayer, and the element of colour that Church ceremonies bring into her otherwise drab life. If she wishes to imagine St This or St That scurrying up to Heaven with her petitions – none of them for herself, all of them for her children or her grandchildren or her neighbours or her lamentable husband – could even a scoundrel of a hack writer wish to deprive her of such innocent comforts? What would her life be without them?

But in some other ways the Church in Ireland is not demanding at all. It may grind Mrs Murphy until her bones crack, but it does not treat her husband in the same way. It does not tell Mr Murphy that if he goes on treating his wife and children the way he does he is likely to end up in Hell. Of course you, sophisticated reader that you are, do not believe in Hell, even for the Mr Murphys of this life, even for the Hitlers. But that is not the point. The Catholic Church *does* believe so; it is only that in Ireland it no longer preaches that it does. It no longer preaches that to avoid going to Hell is very difficult, and that to get to Heaven requires a lifetime of self-sacrifice – or else an inordinate length of time in Purgatory, where the pain is equalled only by the joy of knowing that eventually one will reach God.

Once again, you may yourself dismiss all that as primitive nonsense. But the Catholic Church does not. If it did, it might as well cease to function, for these beliefs are its foundation. These are the things Christ taught in the Gospels. One may choose to disbelieve them, but to do so and to continue to call oneself a Christian and a Catholic is self-deception.

And here *is* the paradox in Irish Catholicism. On a foundation of extreme harshness towards women (and a harshness not at all justified by the Gospels), Irish Catholicism has built a superstructure of extreme tolerance towards the Mr Murphys of Ireland. Partly in fear of losing their allegiance altogether, and partly out of a natural kindliness and tolerance and fellow feeling for masculine foibles.

The result is a strange mixture that, for many young people, presents an unattractive picture. A mixture of indifference to women's pain and an attitude that it is women's role to suffer passively. A failure to demand any *active* idealism, particularly from men. A failure to demand any active self-sacrifice, and to underline the Catholic teaching that that self-sacrifice is essential, now or later – that without it we will never get to Heaven.

As a result, a great many younger people in Ireland are turning away from the Church, simply because it is demanding too little of them. They are looking for a Cross to carry, as the Gospels tell them to, while the Church is offering them the chance to play a guitar at a Folk Mass and to read the lessons.

Of course, the Church will say that any young idealist who wants more than guitar-playing can become a priest or a nun. But even priests and nuns are leaving and the laity – especially the young laity – are leaving. To become atheists, or agnostics, or Zen Buddhists, or Moonies, or Screamers, or Communists, or Young Socialists, or Trotskyites or Born Again Christians, or anything at all that seems to offer them a real and difficult ideal to which they may aspire. (Even atheism is a kind of ideal. It is difficult to stand absolutely alone, without God, in a mechanistic universe.)

Those who are in contact with the kind of young people concerned tell the same story – of disillusionment with a Church and a religion that fails to offer them an ideal to live up to. 'In Dublin I saw people who preached one thing and practised another. They talked about God and thought about money. Here among the Hare Krishnas I am with people who live as they preach, loving and praising God all day.' This from a letter to his anxious Catholic mother by a boy of nineteen who had just joined the cult.

The Hare Krishnas are weird, but they are not hypocrites – at least not at the level young devotees encounter. Too many young Catholics in Ireland are beginning to believe that the Church *is* hypocritical, that it talks about God but thinks about money. And these young people are among the best, the kind who, twenty years ago, *would* have become priests or nuns.

Is it the fault of Vatican Council II?* Or of Humanae Vitae (the much criticised directive of Pope Paul VI that reinforced the long-standing Church ban on all artificial forms of contraception)? Or is it simply the way the world is going, with all authority being called more and more into question and rejected?

If I were obliged to offer an answer I would have to say that the fault lies above all with Vatican II, with the other two playing a part, but a contradictory one.

All three are contradictory, in fact, and yet in some ways similar. All three involved raising Catholic hopes, in Ireland as elsewhere. The Church was going to become a different Church, progressive, liberal, democratic, open to all the winds of change, as a result of Vatican II. There would be a new priesthood, a new kind of religious life, committed to the world's reform and caring for the world's ills in a way that had never been before. There would be a new laity, no longer a simple audience watching the priesthood, but actors in the drama, taking part, sharing the priesthood.

There would be a new kind of bishop, open-minded, listening to his clergy and to his laity. There would be a new kind of Pope, listening to his bishops, listening to his priests, listening to his people. There would be a new kind of Curia, younger, more vital, more sympathetic

* The great council of the Universal Church that sat for several years during the 1960s, intending to draw up a comprehensive scheme of reforms of church discipline, liturgy, and general practice.

to change. There would be a new kind of nun, a part of the 20th century rather than of the 16th. There would be a new role for women in the Church – no longer just as flower-arrangers and bazaar-organisers, but as human beings. And there would be a new role for young people, no longer just as mute recipients of instruction from authority, but as the living seed of the future Church, their voices listened to with respect and interest.

Not much of any of that happened, anywhere. Almost none of it happened in Ireland. In a famous phrase, the then Archbishop of Dublin, John Charles McQuaid, dismissed the whole Vatican Council with all its sittings and all its speeches and all its doctrines and all its documents. 'You have been made anxious about changes,' he said, as he returned to Ireland. 'Nothing will change.'

(Archbishop McQuaid is also justly famous for saying that women athletes undressing beside an athletics racetrack would be an occasion for sin for the male athletes. Accordingly he disapproved of girls or women taking part in any such contests, and the various sporting bodies in the Republic that might otherwise have encouraged women's athletics decided not to. The unwritten episcopal veto has now faded into the past, but an attitude of mind remains that holds that sport is not really the right activity for a woman.)

When he said that nothing would change he was wrong. A great deal changed, but not much of it in the way the best spirits of the Council had hoped. Lay people began reading the lessons. Young people began playing those famous guitars at Mass and singing 'pop' hymns (often atrociously badly, to the distress of the musically minded). Nuns wore shorter skirts and simpler habits. Priests began going about in civilian clothes on their more casual occasions. Here and there lay councils were set up to form a channel between laity and clergy, and priests' committees were set up to form a channel of communication between clergy and hierarchy.

But almost all of this was cosmetic and empty of meaning. And the other side of the coin was disastrous. Disillusioned by the non-events following the high hopes raised by the Vatican Council, priests and nuns began leaving their vocations, with or without the permission of Rome. In Ireland the unthinkable was suddenly happening in almost every parish. Up to the early sixties, the term 'spoiled priest' was one of the most terrible epithets that could be levelled at anyone in Ireland, and a man who left the priesthood (or a nun her convent) was marked with infamy. Suddenly, in the late sixties, it was happening everywhere, faster and faster. Priests were marrying. Nuns were marrying. Sometimes they married each other. The world was surely coming to an end.

An English reader would have to understand the degree of respect and awe in which the Irish clergy were held, and the accompanying expectations and demands exacted of Irish priests and nuns, in order to comprehend the impact of this new phenomenon. Priests could be forgiven a great deal: they could drink too much. But they could not be forgiven for being unchaste, or for turning away from their vocation. Yet now there were so many doing both that they had to be forgiven, or at least overlooked. And there was an atmosphere growing that seemed to imply that the ones who broke their vows were in some peculiar fashion to be applauded, rather than condemned. That *they* were the ones who were liberal and humane and progressive and in the spirit of Vatican II, rather than the reactionary stick-in-the-muds who simply kept on doing what they had promised to do when they were ordained, or when they made their final vows as nuns.

All this had a very disturbing effect on the laity, and the change from the Latin to the English-language Mass exaggerated and underlined the disturbance. Everything seemed different. Women no longer wore hats in church. (Thirty years ago in country parishes men and women in church often sat apart, and no woman would have dared attend Mass without at least a handkerchief over her hair.) Instead of being able to lose oneself in prayer, one was expected to be jumping up and kneeling down and answering the priest, from beginning to end. 'Like the Protestants,' people said. 'And the Folk Masses, with those guitars. And girls wearing jeans. Or mini-skirts. In church! At Mass!'

And out of all this destructive turmoil – nothing, or nothing constructive. It was as though a very old house had been hit with a battering-ram, not once, but several times, so that the mortar fell out from between the bricks and the timbers started, and the slates slid off the joists and the walls cracked. The dust settles, the slates are pushed back in place, but the damage remains.

The next blow of the battering-ram was Humanae Vitae in 1968. Again, the non-Catholic, non-Irish reader needs to understand the expectations raised, and the social background, to understand the disillusion that followed. Catholic teaching in general always favoured large families and frequent childbirth. With the arrival of cheap, commercially produced contraceptives, this teaching was threatened, and in the 20th century Popes more than once condemned their use. In countries with substantial Catholic populations, but where Catholic teaching was not paramount – France, Germany, America, England, Holland – this condemnation was increasingly ignored, simply because under the laws of the countries concerned, contraceptives were easily available.

In Ireland (as in other almost wholly Catholic countries) the situation was different. It was illegal to sell or import for sale contraceptives. As prohibited imports, contraceptive devices could not legally be brought into the country even for private use. If discovered on a traveller, the Customs could and would confiscate them. Of course some were smuggled in, but this smuggling had no real effect on the general situation or atmosphere. Marriage meant children. Lots of children. Only infertility, or abstinence, or coitus interruptus, stood between an Irish Catholic wife and having ten or twelve children in the first fifteen or twenty years of marriage. The poor suffered from this more than the rich – who had access to smuggled sheaths or pills, or who had sympathetic and sophisticated doctors.

Unsophisticated Catholic doctors – or ultra-Catholic doctors – concerned with childbirth were content and even eager to see a working-class woman's body fall to bits rather than tie up her tubes to prevent further pregnancies. And where a doctor in a maternity hospital might have such humane impulses, very often the matron would not, and would prevent it being done. Maternity hospitals were in any event places of terror – some victims claim that they still are, although the horrors have been mitigated over the past twenty years – and everything surrounding pregnancy and childbearing was scarred and shadowed by Irish illogicalities.

On the one hand, children were 'a blessed gift from God', to be welcomed no matter what the cost to the family already overburdened with other 'little gifts'. On the other hand, a woman who was pregnant was described as 'caught', or 'caught again'. There was sometimes a high degree of malice in these phrases, and at other times sympathy. Beneath the 'little gift' attitude there was another, deeper and perhaps more real, an attitude that regarded pregnancy as the curse of Eve, the perennial horror of married life.

Any doctor, any district nurse, knows of cases where a woman who had just given birth would beg them to stay 'just for tonight, nurse, please! Otherwise he'll get into bed with me again, he'll do it again to me. And it hurts so much now.' That, within hours of bearing a child.

Mother of Ten will scream that this is a dirty lie. Establishment Spokesperson will withdraw my passport for the last and final time. But it is not a lie; rather, it is a truth that needs to be told. There are, one must suppose, human animals in the shape of husbands who act like that in every country, but there are not many countries where they can do so and claim the blessing of religion for it.

Of course priests don't approve. But they do nothing about it except utter platitudes regarding moderation and chastity and submitting to the will of God. It is surely not God's will that women should be broken and tortured in the name of 'marriage', and it is surely blasphemy to claim that it could be. It is not so long since priests in confession would ask a woman how it was that after five years of marriage she only had two children. Was she withholding herself from her husband? If she was, that was a sin.

(Catholic attitudes to children as well as to wives could be less than humane. In 1904 – a long time ago in lay terms, but not long in the slow developments of ecclesiastical thought – a Bishop of Ross said that he preferred the cruelty of letting children go hungry to the demoralising effect of giving them free meals in school. And in our own day in the North of Ireland, as well as elsewhere, the hierarchy sets its face against any possibility of Catholic and Protestant children growing up in the same schools, where they might get to know and understand and tolerate one another's religion. By forbidding all such mixing the bishops are condemning another generation of the North's children to the misery of sectarian hatred. It may be theology, but it is not charity, just as condemning women to annual pregnancies and anaemia has no love in it, no matter how many sermons are preached about loving little children, and about the wonderful Catholic family life, modelled on the Family of Nazareth. As the Irish mother of six or seven squalling little snotty-nosed brats said to her parish priest, when he told her to stop complaining and think of the Holy Family, 'Them and their one!')

It was in this atmosphere that the long-awaited Humanae Vitae made its appearance in 1968. Every educated Catholic knew the problem was being discussed, while uneducated Catholics had the feeling that change was coming, was being *promised*. The Pill, the mysterious, wonderful Pill, was going to change everything. Liberal-minded, deeply caring priests were sure that change was coming, and began to hear confessions and grant absolution with that in mind: 'If your conscience *directs* you to use the Pill – or anything else – then God understands. Say a Hail Mary. Pray for me, my child.'

The whole world was going to change. The threat of pregnancy was going to be lifted away from sex. Sex, even in a Catholic marriage, was going to be a joyous thing – or at least, for women long past joy, a tolerable burden.

It was rumoured that the advisory committee of scientists, theologians and lay representatives, appointed by the Pope to study the whole question of contraception, was in favour of change. In an overcrowded world, where the population explosion in poor countries was already threatening disaster, how could it *not* recommend change? The Biblical command 'increase and mulitiply', which stood at the foundation of Catholic family teaching, could no longer apply in a world of 4,000 million people, half of whom were hungry, and millions of whom were starving.

Then came Humanae Vitae, and every hope was cruelly mocked. Nothing was to change. The door that had creaked ajar was slammed shut and locked. The conservatives, laity and priesthood, were delighted. Mother of Ten, freed from the fear that her granddaughter might be a mere Mother of Two, went to Lough Derg on a pilgrimage of thanksgiving. Eighty-year-old bishops who felt that *any* change spelt disaster, and that change in sexual teaching meant the immediate victory of Satan, were relieved. Younger, more liberal clergy and laity were stunned. No single event in 20th-century Catholicism has had such an effect, and such a damaging effect, on Church morale. And the effect was as far-reaching in Ireland as elsewhere. A great many people, even in Ireland, began to see the Church, the 'official' Church, as the enemy of love, and of all humane relationships. Accordingly they abandoned the Church, not because they were bad people, but precisely because they were good people.

The third influence on Irish attitudes to religion in recent years along with Vactican Council II and Humanae Vitae has been that general atmosphere of 'Down with authority' mentioned earlier. In the 1960s people began to reject authority of any kind, often simply because it *was* authority. Not only in politics, but in everything. In fashion, so that women began to wear what they liked, when they liked, and not merely what was fashionable. In education, leading to the student riots of 1968. In popular music, rejecting anything that musical authority regarded as 'musical'. In society, rejecting the old ideals of chivalry and chastity, however little such ideals had ever been observed. Now even the value of those ideals was rejected as being sexist.

Women's rights. Gay rights. Minority rights. All the old moulds were being questioned, and usually broken in the process. Religious moulds were no exception, and Ireland was no exception. Anyone who remembers pre-1960s Ireland finds himself looking back on another world, antediluvian, unrecognisable as the same country of the 1980s.

A great many 'interested parties' will claim that this is not so. That nothing *fundamental* has changed, or at least, not in religion. The conservatives will point to the full churches, Mass attendance, the hysteria over the Papal visit (they will say enthusiasm rather than hysteria), and all the outward signs of an active, vital religious life in Ireland. Liberals will say that there has been a necessary and valuable opening of windows, breaths of much needed fresh air in dusty intellectual corners. They will point to the Folk Masses, the young people who attend them and love them. They will point to the Charismatic Renewal Movement, embracing Protestants as well as Catholics. (The more sophisticated liberals will probably avoid mentioning this extraordinary phenomenon, at which participants often faint in ecstatic trances, and where the atmosphere at the more extreme gatherings is nearer to Bible-Belt America than to old-fashioned Catholicism.)

To offer an opinion on all this turmoil in the once tranquil area of Irish Catholicism would be the height of presumption. Yet having said so much, and implied so much, and then to fail to give a personal opinion would be the depth of cowardice.

Regarding Humanae Vitae, of course the Pope was right to decide as he did, and the people who wanted him to decide differently were wrong. But why did he have to decide at all? Why did he have to raise hopes only to crush them? Why not leave the matter to people's consciences – as has happened, in effect, in most Catholic countries, and as the Church is skilled in doing in areas where it does not want to interfere? Contraception is not like abortion, where another human life is at stake. If a Catholic couple honestly decide they cannot afford, financially or emotionally, to have another child, this affects no one but themselves. Why could Pope Paul VI not have left it like that? Drink does ten thousand times more moral and physical damage in any one day than artificial contraception has done in all the years since it was first invented – if Paul VI wanted to condemn something why did he not condemn drinking? Or over-eating? Or cruelty to women? Or the use of torture in Latin (*Catholic* Latin)-America? Or corruption in American or Italian Catholicism? If he had taken a five-minute Mercedes ride from the Vatican he could have found himself in the worst slums in Europe. Why did he not condemn *them*? In the names of mercy and humanity and common sense, why choose contraception?

And having chosen it, why did he not face the *facts* of too many Catholic marriages? The poverty, the squalor, the hardship, the pain? The swollen bellies and sagging breasts of the Mrs Murphys, the dropped wombs and fallen arches, the varicose veins, the anaemia, the hungry children, the macho husbands demanding their 'rights'? Did he not know them? If he did not, he was not fit to be Pope. Or priest. If he did, why did he not preach against these things?

The real facts are that the 'ideal' Catholic marriage, filled with the love of God, in which sexual abstinence is a joyful thing, in which both partners are absolutely equal, and absolutely united, and are both married to God as much as and more than to each other, and in which they are willing partners in sacrifice – marriages like that are as rare as hen's teeth. The average Catholic marriage, like the average non-Catholic marriage, is a haphazard, harum-scarum affair filled with human pain and only occasionally lightened by human joy. To do anything to make it more painful still seems the work of Satan rather than of the Church of God.

Which brings me back to that third factor that has been loosening the straitjacket of the Church's authority in Ireland, the general post-sixties air of rebellion. When the Pope visited Ireland there was one noticeable event, or rather a pair of events, that people failed to see as being in sharp contrast one with the other. At least, they failed to comment publicly on that contrast. The two events were that the Pope had said 'I love you', at which everyone who heard him fell about in delirium. And that the Pope said 'Men of violence, lay down your arms.' At which the men of violence carried on as if nothing had been said. Yet those men of violence and, more important, their sympathisers, North and South, who make their continuing violence possible, are just as Catholic as the youngsters who shouted with joy when the Pope said he loved them. Catholic Ireland took from the papal visit what it wanted to take, and not what the Pope wanted to give it, which was peace and reconciliation. It took the soft emotions, but not the hard thoughts. It took the flattery, but not the criticism.

And this is one of many reasons why I suspect that the surface, statistical picture of Irish Catholicism, the full churches, the pilgrimages, the novenas, is a false one. That under the smooth surface (and even the surface is not all that smooth) there are subsidence cracks that threaten the whole fabric.

In the years before 1917 – that is, the years before the Revolution – the Russian churches were full, and the full churches in Ireland may therefore be misleading. Well-informed priests calculate that 'There are very real indications in some of our suburban parishes that only 25% to 30% are practising … it would be comforting if all the people came back to church and once again we became a church-going people. But that may not happen.' (The *Sunday Tribune* 22 August 1982, quoting Fr Alec Stenson, in charge of the Dublin Marriage Tribunal, who was addressing the Killarney Conference of Dublin Clergy in 1981.)

According to the same article, the present Archbishop of Dublin, in reality the dominant figure in the Irish hierarchy because of the immense size of his archdiocese when compared to the small country bishoprics, is not seen by most people as the man to reverse this trend away from the Church. He is described as 'obsessed with the maintenance model, as opposed to the missionary model', a one-time liberal who has shed his liberalism on gaining authority, a natural-born bureaucrat who would be more at home in the Curia than in pastoral work. He has also disappointed a great many of his clergy by down-grading and neglecting his 'Council of Priests', once intended as the means by which the junior and parish clergy could share in and help to shape the Church's progress in every diocese. What the Council of Bishops was supposed to be for the Pope (although it has not been), the Councils of Priests were supposed to be for each bishopric, a forum, a democratic body capable of giving advice and criticism to which the bishop would listen attentively. Dr Ryan of Dublin is described as not really a listener: 'He doesn't listen to people. He thinks he's consulting them, but he's really telling them.' Which is fine if what you are telling them is always right, and is clearly right. Unfortunately, more and more people in his archdiocese think he is sometimes wrong.

Of course Dr Ryan is not to be blamed for the fall in numbers attending Mass in his archdiocese, any more than he is for the fall in numbers entering the priesthood. All over the world Catholic statistics have shown a downward trend ever since Vatican Council II. The only increases have been in the numbers of Catholics using contraceptives and getting divorced. Even such conservative organisations as the lay Third Order of St Francis, a pious fraternity of lay men and women and secular clergy founded in 1209 by St Francis of Assisi as a companion order to the First (of Friars vowed to poverty, chastity and obedience) and the Second (of Sisters taking the same vows) have begun to decrease in numbers. In Ireland, where the Third Order has been a major feature of lay piety since the 13th century, membership is now down to 30,000, a considerable drop since the high days of the 1930s, 40s and 50s. (In 1937, for instance, 5,000 members of the Third Order were present on one single pilgrimage to the Shrine at Knock.)

The present organisers of the Third Order in Ireland consider the fall in numbers as bringing 'its own positive result – a whole new look at the importance of quality ... ' rather than of quantity. The sad fact remains that the young and enthusiastic are looking elsewhere, and the attitude of mind exemplified in Ireland by

Archbishop Ryan – which critics have stigmatised as seeing the Church's problems 'in terms of staffing rather than missionary zeal,' is not helping matters. The whole glory of Irish Catholicism, from the time of St Patrick, was its missionary and pastoral zeal. To concentrate on turning it into a smooth-running, well staffed bureaucracy is to miss the point of it, and utterly to diminish it.

5 Women

Broadly speaking, the Irish masculine presumption is that a woman is property. That she likes being property, and that lacking a man to own her and abuse her and order her about she will become neurotic. That she is much stupider than men, and greedier and more materialistic than men. That her mental processes are confined to thinking about having babies and furnishing a house. That if a man lets a woman have too much of her own way he is not a man at all, while she will become a tyrant. That for a women to be in any position of authority over a man is against nature. That a woman's proper place is on her back, and that she only respects a man capable of putting her there, will-she, nill-she. That when women are raped they were really asking for it.

But over against this, and hinted at within its framework, there is another view of women that is almost an opposite. That woman is a monster, whose ambition is to destroy and devour men. That a woman will suck a man dry like a vampire if he gives her half a chance. That a man's only hope of escape is to stay in the warm, comradely company of other men – pub friends, fellow drinkers, fellow football players – because only in masculine fraternity and unity and solidarity is here any safety against the horrid magic of the Ban Shee, the Hag, the Seductress.

There is also a third Irish masculine view of woman, that of her as Mother, a subtle blend of the two foregoing images, and varying now towards the one and now towards the other: the family tyrant grasping limp and bloodless sons and husbands against her monstrous breasts; and the loving, all-enduring victim willing to feed her (male) children on her heart's blood.

On the other side of the coin there is the feminist view of Irish women as exploited slaves, discriminated against by law, by society, by tradition; brutalised, robbed of dignity, denied even minimal human rights, told what to do and what not to do, even in bed, by men. Even their bodies do not belong to them. A physical assault against a woman is not regarded in the same way, by law or society, as is an assault against a man. The guards will not protect them. There are societies for protecting dogs and cats and children from cruelty, but there is none to protect women. Women are not second-class citizens. They are slaves. Outcasts.

Finally there is the reality, which surely must embrace some fragments at least of some of these descriptions. But who – least of all a man – is to say what that reality is? Yet in a book supposedly about Ireland some attempt must be made, however foredoomed. Let it be said, then, first and foremost and in a faint and probably hopeless attempt to turn away wrath, that the feminist view is the nearest to the truth – as one might expect. And yet in many ways women do play a dominating role in Irish *domestic* life, and through that role they help to give a distinctive shape to Irish public life

But before considering the unsatisfactory status of modern Irish women, it might be interesting to glance briefly at what used to be women's status in Gaelic Ireland.

Until the end of the 17th century large parts of Ireland remained under the influence of Gaelic Law, known properly as the Brehon Laws, from the Irish word for a judge. And these laws seem to have accorded something much nearer to equality for women than either Church law or English law, both of which systems competed with Gaelic law in Ireland for the obedience of the population.

English law was paramount, naturally, wherever English political authority was paramount. This area varied through the centuries from the Norman invasion of the 12th century to the final subjection of the West of Ireland following the defeat of the deposed King James II of England and his Lieutenant Patrick Sarsfield in 1690 and 1691, after which the Penal Laws were imposed upon the whole country without exception, discriminating harshly against Catholics. Church law, on the other hand, theoretically held sway throughout Ireland from the time of the country's first Christianisation under Palladius and St Patrick, and was applied to all those aspects of Irish life which were proper to it, exactly as in Catholic England before the Reformation.

Church law, however, seems to have had a very tenuous hold in Ireland in regard to anything that concerned the family and, therefore, anything that concerned the status of women. Divorce, for example, was easy, and from the evidence of various medieval Irish chronicles women seem to have exercised a right to claim divorce whenever it suited them, on an apparently equal footing with men. This was made possible by the custom of civil rather than religious marriage. A 16th-century observer, Sir John Popham, the Attorney-General in England and therefore for the English-held area of Ireland, claimed that only about one out of twenty Irish marriages took place in a church.

The unions that did take place varied from the most casual and promiscuous affairs to real marriages of intent, which later the Church recognised, without having been asked to bless them. But these more stable civil marriages were often not monogamous. There are records of men with several wives all at the one time and, more interesting to this particular argument, of women with several husbands. There was also a custom by which the mother of an illegitimate child could 'name' the father. She very often 'named' a great man of the district, not really as an accusation, but as an appeal for the 'named' man to take an interest in her child, which very often he did, on the basis of noblesse oblige. (He must also have often been unsure as to whether or not he might truly have been the father, because it was an accepted custom that chiefs spread their favours far and wide among their followers.) Such children were, once accepted, considered to be of noble blood, for there was no inequality between 'legitimate' and 'illegitimate' children under Brehon Law; all offspring had equal rights in matters of inheritance.

There was, in general, an approach to sex and marriage among the medieval Irish that the English found extremely reprehensible. Even the clergy were affected by the prevailing atmosphere of libertarianism, and two bishops of the 14th century are on record not merely as possessing wives, but as having pledged Church lands to these wives as marriage gifts. (At the same time as receiving a marriage gift from her husband a wife received a dowry from her own family, originally in the form of cattle, but by the 16th century in money. This dowry was paid to her husband, but in the case of divorce was to be repaid to her, or more probably to her family.)

It is easier to state these facts than to interpret them. In the first place, the people named in the chronicles as taking advantage of these laws and customs were usually of noble birth while how the lower classes behaved was rarely considered worth describing. One can, however, be reasonably certain that they were no more puritanical than their betters. The whole drift and atmosphere of Gaelic literature and legend is of an attitude to sex almost diametrically opposed to that of English law – where sexual laxity threatened property rights – and of Church law – where it threatened Church authority. For Gaelic Ireland sex was a joyous matter.

This explains some part of the ferocious enmity felt by English observers against the Irish, which was not unlike that of readers of the *Daily Telegraph* commenting on a hippy pop music festival in their neighbourhood – a mixture of fear and sexual jealousy.

But a free-wheeling attitude to sex does not necessarily mean a satisfactory status for women. Hippy girls often seemed to be the abject slaves of their hippy male protector, not *more* free than their bourgeois counterparts, but less so. Even their long, draggled skirts indicated retrogression rather than an advance into a free and glorious future. Were Gaelic women mere sex objects?

One can only say that this does not seem to have been so. One noblewoman of the 14th century was not only called 'the Great', but also nicknamed 'the meeting place of the three enemies' because she was married, at the same time, to three chieftains, each the sworn enemy of the other two. She was also married to other men and, as I have said, this multiple marriage by women was not uncommon. Neither was it a 14th-century aberration – Queen Maebh of Connaught of the Iron Age legends was known for her 'hospitable thighs'.

Of course, some great ladies in every society have been loose-living. But in Gaelic Ireland this was not a hushed-up departure from a more sedate norm, but an accepted way of life. There was neither sniggering nor condemnation involved, it was simply 'how things were'. And it seems impossible to interpret the known facts in any way that suggests that women in Gaelic Ireland were worse off than they became later, when Church and English law laid firm hold on their affairs. Indeed, one could imagine that a part of the Church's suspicion of Irish womanhood derives from fear, a fear that, if given the chance, Irish women might again ignore the trammels of Christian subjection and thus destroy the Church's influence.

Christian propagandists would claim that, with the gradual imposition of monogamy and the ideal of pre-marital chastity and devotion to the Virgin Mary as 'Woman par excellence', the Church did not diminish the status of women but improved it. It is, however, very hard to accept this. Even the evidence of the New Testament offers a picture of women exercising more influence and enjoying more freedom than their later counterparts. A number of Jewish women were clearly free to wander round Palestine accompanying Our Lord, and even the Pharisees found nothing to criticise in this. They evidently thought it permissible. And St Paul on his journeys repeatedly speaks of the 'influential' women of this town and that, and from whom he received help. (At one point he speaks of a 'deaconess', a reference later writers have taken pains to dismiss as not meaning what it says – that a woman held an important position of authority in a church).

It seems sad, but it is nevertheless true, that wherever Christianity has spread (just as wherever Mahommedanism has spread) the status of women has become even less endurable than it was before. It is equally evident that this was never the intention of the founder of Christianity (or of Mahommedanism). The Gospels, like the Koran, like even St Paul in his epistles, speak of women with respect and love, and where they impose obligations on women towards men, they impose equally strict obligations on men towards women. But men, who control both religions, choose to be selective in applying this advice.

The situation of Irish women today needs to be seen in the light of this background. It also needs to be seen in the light of the strong belief in breeding which the Irish have. For although, as I have mentioned earlier, we tend to be suspicious of class, we think a great deal of 'good stock'. We also think a great deal of money, and it was not so long ago that the farmer's son married the neighbour's daughter, when he was allowed to marry at all (very often he wasn't, for marriage meant a second woman in the house and pressure on the father to hand over the farm to his new-married son) he was allowed to marry not because of her looks, but because of her 'breeding', and her dowry. Let her have a hump-back and squint, but 'she comes of good, sound stock, and has a power of money in the bank.' In the old days a 'power of money' could be a hundred pounds, and if she brought a cow or two along with that she could take her pick of husbands. If she had nothing, then a joyous figure and a gladsome eye could leave her a spinster for ever.

And this materialistic approach to marriage – peasant rather than Irish – has had effects that have lasted until today. I have known beautiful girls wither and languish in Dublin, unasked in marriage – not even asked out with dishonourable intentions in mind. The more beautiful they were, the more neglected. Men were simply afraid of them. Afraid of being tempted into an irrational marriage. Afraid of a partner who outshone them in looks and sex appeal. Afraid of possessing something that other men might want, and thus try to take. Over the same period I have seen relatively handsome men choose the most extraordinarily plain brides (at one moment I threatened to keep a cuttings book of really woeful wedding photographs from the Irish papers, but the project seemed too sadistic).

Part of the answer has to be that a great many Irishmen feel extremely insecure. They want a partner they can dominate and neglect, and who will put up with anything because she is so grateful for marriage. Was it Boswell who said that he always chose middle-aged women for his attentions because they were so grateful? Irishmen seem often to work on the same principle. And too many of them do neglect their wives. They give them too many children too quickly, find the pressures of marriage too great and the attractions too few, and retreat to the pub.

Some husbands also take their revenge on women by wife-beating – as they do in England and America and elsewhere – and others simply abandon their wives and escape to England. There are no official figures for deserted wives (any more than for battered wives) in Ireland, but there are claimed to be about 50,000 single-parent families here, a very large number for a very small country, and the greater proportion of those will be married women whose husbands went out to post a letter or to find a job, and never came back.

It would obviously be wrong to say flatly that 'Irishmen make bad husbands'. Irishmen are as various as anyone else. But if one were to reverse the claim, and attempt to say that 'Irishmen make good husbands', a hollow derisive laugh followed by a cry of rage would rise from every feminist organisation in Ireland. The following extract from a social worker's report on a battered wife – a woman from an 'educated' family who married 'beneath' her, in this case – illustrates vividly what happens when a husband feels insecure:

I'm supposed to wear glasses. I'm short-sighted. He doesn't allow me read. He can't bear to see me reading even at night. He says if I have library books that I'll read all day. So he broke my glasses and the last time he danced on them and I had to shovel them up and he wouldn't allow me get another set of glasses. It's awful up here in Dublin. I can't see the numbers on the buses or anything. I have a free doctor, but nothing else, so I couldn't get my own glasses. Anyway, the first he goes for is my glasses. I'm not allowed any books or papers or anything. That's what started this rumpus. I went down to the library and stupidly got out two books and he found them, and he nearly killed me. I couldn't even say news I'd read or he would know I'd read the paper. And if he got the paper he'd bundle it up and put it in the bottom of the bin so I couldn't read it.

He is self-educated and he can discuss on' any subject. But any reference to studies or sums or anything he can't do it. I asked him to do a sum because he's supposedly more intelligent than me. So he got up very slowly and shut the door, and then he came back and said, 'Now I'm going to spatter your grey matter on the ceiling.' He had me down on the ground, and said, 'Now are you going to do what you're told?' I was only back in the house two hours at the time.

No one could call that a 'typical Irish marriage', but it happens too often, and not simply among the working-classes. And Irish law and

Irish judges are either ill equipped or unwilling to intervene on the woman's behalf, as a further extract from the same social worker's notebook illustrates.

We may start by asking what happens in court if a woman decides to charge her husband. If she actually goes through with the whole procedure of charging her husband which she rarely does, the husband may then be fined, bound to the peace, have his case adjourned, be imprisoned or referred by the court for medical report. In assault cases District Justices have the power at their own discretion to refer the defendant in custody for a psychiatrist's report and to refuse bail if there is a clear indication that he will perpetrate further violence against his wife. These powers, despite evidence of a husband's murderous intent against his wife, are seldom if ever invoked and bail is almost invariably granted. (District Justice Delap is an exception here, and is known to show considerable understanding in marital cases in his court.)

We must point out here that the husband is a defendant on a criminal charge and is entitled to claim free legal representation from the state. But the wife, as witness or plaintiff, is not entitled to this unless she is lucky enough to live in the Dublin area and can avail of the services of the free legal aid centres.

Unfortunately, the possibilities open to the judges are not great. He can send the man to prison and he does sometimes do this, but the man usually appeals, staying all the time free in the meantime, and more often than not the man gets off on appeal. One husband who was caught chasing his wife down the quays in Dublin with a hatchet in his hand in 1974 was given a 3 months sentence, and the sentence was eventually suspended on appeal. This man had been seen by a squad car which then stopped and interfered. He immediately proceeded to attack the police car.

A three month suspended sentence for attempting to murder one's wife in public, and for attacking a police car with a hatchet, seems to be very lenient indeed. Such leniency shown in a domestic case implies nothing more than the basic approval of a male judge for the behaviour of this extrovert and very violent husband.

'Too many busybodies interfering in marriage cases.'* This was one judge's commentary concerning a case where one of the women living in the refuge brought charges against her husband for battery and assault. Her husband had stabbed her in the neck and arm with a screwdriver. She told the judge that she was terribly frightened, and that ever since she had been staying with Women's Aid refuge. It was explained to the judge that there had been other assaults on divers occasions and that the attack in question was provoked, because the woman had been unable to get his asthma tablets from the doctor. Justice McCarthy adjourned the case for 3 months to allow the couple to settle their differences. He noted that 'Mr ... was asthmatic and needed tablets for health reasons', and he then said, 'Your marriage problems are your own affair'. He went on to warn 'busybodies' not to interfere in going to help cases which had difficulties. He added, 'There are too many people in this country and particularly in Dublin prepared to interfere with people's business when it does not concern them.' He suggested that the couple should try to settle their problems together. This advice would have been all very well if the woman in question were not absolutely terrified of her husband. The judge sent them off thinking they were going home together to settle their differences. In fact, the woman went straight back to the refuge, to those 'busybodies' who are interfering in people's marriages. The woman herself told me she had no choice. She could not attempt to live away from the refuge while her husband was free to walk the streets.

If the law is unhelpful, what about society? The newspapers? Neighbours? The local priests?

The fact is that the newspapers have ignored up to recently, and still do to a large extent, the enormous conflict that can exist between husband and wife. The problem is also ignored in

* *Irish Independent*, 19 August 1975.

the same way by the neighbours, the parish priest, the social agencies, supposedly responsible, and up and up until one can say that the whole of society practically speaking chooses to ignore that a problem exists and that women do get beaten, sometimes to death, by their husbands. This silence can only be one of tacit approval, otherwise such phenomena would not be tolerated. Here I note certain newspaper headings pointed out to me at Women's Aid concerning cases of which they had more detailed knowledge, and which I find rather indicative of this tacit approval, brought out by the deliberate choice to censor the information give to the public.

'Man helping police with their enquiries' and 'Woman found dead in a pool of blood'. These were the newspaper headings of April, 27th [1976] concerning the death of a woman who had been beaten all her married life. The neighbours knew, the police knew, the Social Workers knew, and yet the newspapers published nothing resembling the truth. It would appear that battering one's wife is a secret, unwritten right of the husband, that up to recently was not even talked about or admitted to exist, let alone complained about.

Three days before her death the woman in question was severely battered on a Sunday morning. Her husband then left her lying in a pool of blood, and went off until the following day. It was the neighbours who noticed their little boy and girl wandering aimlessly in the street. They went into the house, to find the mother lying in a coma. The woman was rushed to Harcourt Street Hospital in Dublin in a critical state. At this stage the neighbours, taken by their conscience, rang up the refuge for battered housewives to ask them to keep in touch with the hospital, and were told that the woman was as well as could be expected, and that her husband was at her bedside.

The woman died two days later, and the husband was allowed to go back home to look after the children. The police did not think fit to arrest him. The reaction from the neighbours was so strong that they were finally obliged to.

In another case, the refuge was informed by a parish priest from Galway, who taken by his conscience could no longer keep silent. I am not permitted in this case to give dates, places or names. As in so many other crimes committed in domestic circumstances, it is shrouded in a mist of silence. The case in question was a simple one of suicide, according to the newspapers. A woman with her two small children and 15-month old baby threw herself and the children over a cliff, to a certain death. The bodies were washed up on the shore the following day. At the inquest it was said that she had been depressed for some time. The husband appeared at the funeral in tears and all in black, with his mother at his side to support him.

The parish priest who wrote to the refuge begging their silence at the same time, told them that this woman had been systematically beaten and badly treated throughout the five years of her marriage, and that living in a small and hostile community with no money of her own, her one and only outlet was death. This is all we know about the case. But it does not sound very different from so many other cases described by women who instead of committing suicide come to the refuge. Their stories are each time a tale of the complicity that exists between their husbands and society around them. In Mary's case, we notice the attitude of the police, the way they tell her to go home and to do it 'their' way, that is to go back and get 'battered' again. It's not enough to be simply battered for the police, they seem to want something more before making an arrest. We have seen that even the woman's death may not be enough to provoke an arrest.

Even when a woman presses charges against her husband it is not at all evident that the police will arrest him. This fact seemed to escape one policeman with whom I talked when he remarked to me that women nearly always withdraw their charges. The fact is that it is very difficult for the woman if she has to spend the night before going to court, with her husband, who may bully her or persuade her with promises, into withdrawing. But if the police do arrest the husband, the woman may still fail to go through with the court procedure out of pure blind fear that her husband will be released the following morning, which is what happens more often than not. If he can be released on bail within a matter of hours by his friends or relations it is not surprising that she doesn't press her charges, and when he gets a suspended sentence it is even less surprising that she doesn't try a second time.*

How many Irish wives are battered, as a commonplace occurrence, during their marriage? No one knows. Until a few years ago, when Women's Aid (an organisation formed in the early 1970s to help battered wives) began to explore the problem, no one wanted to know. The problem is still not a popular one for discussion, least of all by the government departments most concerned, those of Justice and Health.

A very rough indication can be got from the number of women who apply to Women's Aid for shelter. In 1981, 373 women sought refuge in the Dublin hostel alone. At any one moment, that year and since, there have been on average 26 women and 70 children resident there. If there was more accommodation the figures would undoubtedly be higher.

Nor are these figures more than a minimal indication of the size of the problem. Many wives never seek refuge with Women's Aid. They run away. They continue to endure. Or they die. And no one, often not even their own families, knows what has been happening; the victims are too ashamed to tell. They go to great lengths, endless lengths, to conceal what is happening. Others simply accept being beaten as a fact of married life. Their fathers battered their mothers, and they expect their husbands to beat them. There is even an element of pride in being beaten, in some cases. It seems to the victim to be a proof of the husband's virility.

And of course Women's Aid is mainly concerned with working-class victims. But this does not mean that only working-class wives are battered. It is equally a problem in the middle-classes, although few, if any, middle-class wives could stand the atmosphere of the hostel, and wherever they seek refuge it is not there. Once a middle-class woman makes up her mind to escape from a husband's violence she is likely to have more opportunities of finding a relative or a friend able and willing to help her, more access to the essential

* I am grateful to my daughter Tanga Quinn for these quotations from her casebook and MA thesis.

minimum of money necessary for an escape, more knowledge of the legal and social resources open to her, few as they are. A working-class wife who is battered may go to the Guards and find no help there. A middle-class wife in the same crisis is more likely to turn to a solicitor and receive practical assistance in the form of a court injunction.

Nevertheless, a great many middle-class victims, like their working-class sisters, seek no help or, failing to receive such help at first, look no further. They endure or die. For untold numbers of wives of every social level the walls of the family home form a prison within which mental and physical torture are a daily occurrence. Hell can be a corporation flat or a semi-detached estate house, or a villa in an expensive suburb; the wife-batterer can be a professional man as easily as a labourer. And except for a few dedicated feminists and reformers, no one wishes to hear a word about it.

Why does it happen? Why do large numbers of men in Ireland, Catholic Ireland, beat their wives, and not simply beat them, but batter them, kick them, break their bones, stab them, and sometimes kill them? The answer cannot lie in some purely Irish factor, because it happens elsewhere. But *how* can it happen in a country where devotion to the Virgin Mary is one of the most powerful elements in popular religion? Where respect for motherhood is supposedly a national characteristic?

The answer has to be that whatever the Church teaches, and whatever society pretends to believe, the atmosphere of Irish society is, if not hostile to women, contemptuous of them. Women are not fully human. Women deserve to be beaten, and *need* to be beaten, to keep them in their place and to teach them how to be good wives.

Of course, any defender of Ireland's good name will reject this out of hand as a horrible slander, pointing to the vast majority of Irish husbands who do not beat their wives. Big deal. Until wife-battering is regarded with the same horror as any other violent crime, and condemned as the bestial cruelty that it is, Irish society must accept the stigma of tolerating it. And by tolerating it, condoning it. And by condoning it, approving it.

Is it grossly unfair to mention such cases? To offer them as any sort of example of Irish marriage? As any sort of illustration of Irish society? Or of Irish attitudes to women? Most men will say 'Yes! Not only unfair, but vicious, unpatriotic, a travesty of the truth, which is that 99 per cent of Irish marriages are happy, or at least satisfactory.' But a great many women, and I think all feminists, will accept it as very fair, and they would hoot with scorn at that claim of 99 per cent of successful marriages.

My justification for including these cases – as it will be for including some other uncomfortable facts elsewhere in this book – is that the Irish Establishment from de Valera onwards has pumped out so much hypocritical propaganda about the happy and holy state of Irish marriage that if one is to mention it at all one must underline the shadows. The position of women in most 'civilised' countries is pretty bleak. In Ireland, because of that time-lag mentioned earlier, it has been bleaker than in most other comparable countries.

It remains unhappier than it needs to for several reasons which are peculiarly Irish. In Ireland there is no divorce, and contraception – although now legally, if grudgingly, recognised – is sometimes hard to come by. Until quite recently it was impossible to come by at all without breaking the law.

Alone among the countries of Europe Ireland forbids divorce. And it not only forbids civil divorce, it even refuses to recognise Church annulments. These have been granted, slowly and with difficulty, over the last five years for example, at the rate of about ninety-five a year. (A typical annulment case might take three years and cost two or three hundred pounds, but cases have been known to linger on for ten and fifteen years, by which time the recipients of the decree are often past caring.) In the same period, about forty petitions were rejected each year, making a total of 135 aplications per year for annulments. One must, of course, add to this figure a varying number of people per year who are turned down even before their applications become formal, as possessing no grounds for the applications to be pursued, while there are others who simply do not pursue their applications.

Obviously, this represents only a fraction of the number of Irish couples whose marriages have effectively ceased to have any meaning. Moreover, even this small fraction gets no recognition from the Irish state. Article 41, Section 2 of the Irish Constitution reads, 'No Law shall be enacted providing for the grant of a dissolution of marriage'. Whatever the intentions of those who drafted this section, the result is that annulments are not recognised as having validity within the Republic. No civil dissolution of an annulled marriage can follow an annulment which is, therefore, theoretically useless to those who receive it. Of course in fact, as opposed to theory, the people concerned can and often do re-marry other partners elsewhere, but the theory remains, and on returning to Ireland they are – again theoretically – guilty of bigamy. The state has never prosecuted any such case, but the possibility remains, and many problems can arise for such individuals over inheritances. In the eyes of the law they are still married to the previous partner, who can claim their estate when they die. Ireland is the only Catholic country where such anomalies exist, a singularity which amuses those unaffected by it, infuriates those who are, and appears to leave the government not only indifferent but determined to create further such singularities whenever the opportunity occurs.

This 'holier than Rome' attitude to divorce is enshrined in the Irish Constitution, and that brings me to another Irish peculiarity – one of those small differences that really do exist – which some enthusiasts want to see also enshrined in the Constitution. This is a veto on abortion. Abortion is already illegal in Ireland, as one might expect, and there are no exceptions to this illegality. Girls and women who want or who believe that they need abortions go to England for them, at a present rate of several thousand a year. No constitutional amendment will stop them doing it, but in 1981 the aforementioned group of enthusiasts petitioned the then Taoiseach, Mr Charles Haughey, to introduce a referendum calling for an amendment to the Constitution in which the illegality of abortion would be fixed for ever, with no risk that it might ever be made legal (as has happened in England and in other countries). Mr Haughey agreed. His enemies said he was electioneering.

His friends are convinced that he sees abortion as a deep moral danger. As well he might; as indeed it is. The Irish peculiarity – the Irish dimension, as an English politician might say – is that no one, no one at all, no body of opinion, no pressure group, no subversive organisation, has ever proposed that abortion should be made legal here. Even the women most concerned, the unwillingly pregnant, are not asking for legalised Irish abortions. They are sadly content to receive legalised English ones.

Then why this sudden and highly vocal concern? No one knows. A small group started making a large outcry, obtained Mr Haughey's agreement to call a referendum on the matter, and the outcry has continued on a long crescendo ever since. The Dublin papers' Letters to the Editor columns have sometimes seemed to be concerned with nothing else. The Churches have become involved, as have political parties, women's groups, and Northern politicians (for whom the Southern Constitution has significance, whether they are for or against it).

A further oddity is that everyone concerned in the uproar is on the same side, which makes for even fiercer disagreement. The pro-amendment people are against abortion and pro-life. The anti-amendment people are against abortion and pro-life. The difference is that these see no point in spending £800,000 (at 1982 prices) on a referendum which is totally unnecessary, which will change nothing, and which will fail to protect so much as one foetus. They also see the proposed amendment as sectarian, underlining in an offensive – and again absolutely unnecessary – manner, the dominant position of the Catholic Church in Southern Ireland.

At the time of writing the conflict is still unresolved. By the time you read this no doubt it will have been solved, by Mr Haughey producing another uniquely Irish solution to an Irish problem – unless he loses a general election in the meantime. (As he did, shortly after this was written. But a change of government is unlikely to make much difference to this turmoil in a tea cup. The solution may be different, but it will be equally bizarre – and unsatisfactory.)

And then there is contraception. Until 1980 the sale, or importation for sale, or advertising of artificial means of contraception other than the Pill were all illegal in the Irish Republic. (The Pill was and remains regarded as a legitimate means of regulating a woman's periods, and its contraceptive effects were and remain disregarded.)

Following a lengthy legal case brought against the State, in 1972-3, by a married couple on the grounds that the then situation was unconstitutional, by depriving the couple of the right to regulate their family according to their own consciences and by the means their medical adviser thought best, the government of the day undertook to amend the law. The result appeared in 1979 as the

Health (Family Planning) Act, described by its author and begetter, Mr Haughey, as an Irish solution to an Irish problem. Which indeed it was.

Instead of saying, as a less imaginative man and government might have said, that 'this is a matter for a citizen's individual conscience. Let the things be imported and sold', the Act went into mild contortions about who might and who might not import contraceptives, sell them, use them, prescribe them, and even make them. (Equally imaginative Irish citizens had been using 'cling film' for the purpose, cling film being more normally used for wrapping food for the fridge.) In essence, the Act provided that contraceptives should be available on prescription from chemists. But the doctor who made out the prescription had to be satisfied that the patients 'sought the contraceptives for the purpose, bona fide, of family planning or for adequate medical reasons and in appropriate circumstances'.

The Act was greeted with a mixture of ridicule and outrage. Ridicule from those graceless souls who believe that what a man and woman, or even a boy and girl, do in bed is their business, and not that of the Minister for Justice, or even of the Minister for Health. And outrage from the *bien pensants*, who feel that all erections need to be controlled by the Minister for the Environment and given planning permission only with the most stringent safeguards.

Not only citizens – and citizenesses – were divided in this way. Doctors, called on to act as arbiters – is Willy Murphy, 17-year-old skinhead, *really* a bona fide family planner? – felt, quite legitimately one thinks, that such decisions were outside the terms of the Hippocratic Oath, now to be restyled the Hypocritic Affirmation. '16-year-old Eliza Murphy is in my opinion in genuine need of family planning and is a proper person to be allowed to buy 6 (six) only Durex sheaths, the medicament to be used once nightly.'

Chemists, a conservative lot by nature, felt that the government was insisting that Satan should have a hand in their business, and rebelled *en masse*. The results, two years into the new era of Irish permissiveness, are summed up in the following extracts from an article in the *Sunday Tribune* of 29 August 1982:

'IRISH SOLUTION' FAILS TO SOLVE CONTRACEPTION PROBLEM

Two years after the Family Planning Bill introduced by Mr. Haughey (as Minister for Health) became law, Emily O'Reilly and Geraldine Grennan reveal that the Act is now a dead letter.

The controversial Health (Family Planning) Act of 1979 has now been in operation for almost two years. The Department of Health is presently reviewing its operation. We can save them the trouble. Our investigation shows that:

Only 15% of Irish chemists stock contraceptives other than the pill (they are the sole legitimate suppliers under the act).

80% of contraceptives used here are supplied illegally by private clinics.

Three major clinics are operating without the licence required under the act (even for an advice service).

None of the Health Boards has provided its own family planning service available locally.

Overall, there is no sign that the passage of the act has had any significant effect.

Correspondence subsequent to this article revealed the presence in Ireland of approximately one hundred centres run by NAOMI (National Association of the Ovulation Method of Ireland), at which instruction was given in the Billings ovulation method of natural family planning. But, as the *Sunday Tribune* reporter pointed out, these centres were not listed in the Golden Pages of the telephone directory, and their existence was not well known.

But let the final word on such matters come from ALLY, the organisation founded to help unmarried mothers-to-be during pregnancy. 'Many parents go to great lengths to impress on their daughters the seriousness of getting pregnant outside marriage, but they seem to neglect to talk to their sons about sexual responsibility.' The result is that two-thirds of unmarried fathers whose partners have approached ALLY for help abandoned the girl completely and left her to cope with her pregnancy as best she could alone. And 65 per cent of these girls are twenty-one or under, with almost half of them afraid to tell their parents.

(In mid-1983, after two and a half years of the non-working of the 'Irish Solution', the new government is promising new legislation to introduce a breath of rationality into the matter.)

Abortion. Contraception only on a doctor's prescription. Wife battering. It would be pleasant to be able to claim that in spite of all this Irish women are gaining equality of status. And in some areas they really are, compared to the Victorian situations of even thirty years ago. Women drive cars, have bank accounts, careers, increasing independence. They speak out more and more on things that concern women as a sex. But they still play a noticeably small part in public affairs. There is never more than a handful of women in the Dáil, eight at present,* and women councillors are equally rare, in town or country. No woman has ever held an important ministry (the one most recently occupying any ministerial position has just been demoted). No one expects to see a woman Taoiseach, in this or any foreseeable decade, or a woman President. Women are not prominent in business. No semi-state body has a woman senior executive (or if one has, it's a well kept secret). No national newspaper has a woman editor (as opposed to a woman editor of the women's page), and no one expects to see one. There is no highly placed woman in Telefís Eireann or Radio Eireann. No voice has been raised in modern Ireland for women to become priests. Women starting out on any career are discriminated against by their male employers or by directors on the ground that 'women never stay. They leave to get married as soon as you've trained them.'

But I suspect that this is a negative picture, which could be discovered in England and many other countries as easily as in Ireland. There is nothing particularly Irish about it. What is perhaps more Irish is that among the staunchest supporters of the status quo in all these regards are women themselves. Not all women of course, but some, and not just a few. Mother of Ten has a frightening number of female allies, who for any of many reasons do not want things changed.

(I'm sorry if reference to Mother of Ten seems like masculine prejudice. Of course there have to be men willing to co-operate or even to insist before any woman can become a Mother of Ten, or of any. A few years ago there was one briefly notorious man in Dublin

---

* In the new Dáil, following our last election, the figure has risen to fourteen, but this is still less than 10 per cent of the total. In Ireland, as elsewhere, women fail to vote for women.

who boasted publicly of being the Father of Eighteen, all by the same delighted wife – at least, he claimed she was delighted. But in general Fathers of Ten are rather shy of publicity. One imagines them worn out by their exertions and seeking only the friendly refuge of a favourite pub. And, to be entirely serious about an immensely serious subject, most Mothers of Ten – and Mothers of Five or Four or Three, for that matter – are also worn out by their exertions, with no public house to give them comfort unless they want to be branded as monsters. Nevertheless, 'Mother of Ten' has for a long time played a part in Ireland's folklore, as the ferocious guardian of public morals. I humbly apologise to everyone for mentioning the matter.)

It is also the case in a great many Irish families that mothers give a quite different upbringing to their sons than to their daughters. The sons are spoiled. The daughters are enslaved. The sons are given every opportunity to do their homework. The daughters are expected to help with the housework when they get home from school. When they are old enough to go to work the sons keep their wages 'because they need them, being boys'. The girls give theirs up 'because that's right, it'll teach them to manage,' and they get a fraction back as pocket money. There are families where girls are expected to clean the boys' shoes and cook their suppers and iron their shirts and make their beds.

Of course, this is not a universal picture, and less so than it was even ten or twenty years ago. And there are plenty of young girls who would be better off for more discipline instead of less, as there are boys. But this discrimination still exists, and it is applied and retained by women rather than men, because on the whole the mother sets the tone of the average family and decides who does what and who receives what and who is denied what. If Irish boys are spoiled brats and grow up to be rotten husbands, nine times out of ten it was their mothers who spoiled them, laying up future horrors and hardships for another woman.

And, just as in traditional – or mythical – Jewish families, there is an equivocal relationship between Irish mothers and their sons, a possessiveness that can easily turn unhealthy. A woman with an unsatisfactory husband turns for compensation to her son. The husband is a lost cause, but the son will make up for it and, in return, be given everything. Love. Adoration. A blind eye to faults. The result can be ruinous in one of several ways: an emasculated homosexual; a tyrant ready to exploit his wife as he has been taught to exploit his mother; a soured bachelor always looking for a woman like his mother, meaning a female doormat who can cook, and never finding one to his taste; a shallow philanderer who regards all women as mother-substitutes, existing only to wash his socks and warm his bed; a tearful drunk, lamenting mother machree, and the decline of womanhood and female chastity. It is scarcely possible to sketch the outline of an Irish monster, selfish, vain, drunken, lecherous, feeble, and not realise that the original was created by an Irish mother.

Moreover, if Irishmen – young Irishmen – behave extraordinarily badly in ordinary social life and in boy-girl relationships, as an enormous number of them do, why do the girls put up with it? Why do they wait patiently until the pubs close for the boy to stagger out with them and pay them some sort of attention? Why do they lend their boy-friends money (at the starting point of many careers girls can earn more than boys in Ireland, as perhaps they can in England) and provide them with meals at home, and invite them in for the night when they know beforehand that the boy is next-door to useless as a potential husband, or else has no intention of becoming a husband, and in any event is a boorish lout, unfit to be any kind of companion?

The girls complain bitterly about the boys, but they go on submitting to them, and spoiling them, and excusing them. The boys in turn say that all that the girls are interested in is the deposit on a house and a wedding ring and furniture, and that they will go to any lengths to secure them, regardless of the poor Guinness-sodden wretch who is blackmailed into providing the means.

(ESTABLISHMENT SPOKESPERSON: I can't stand another word of this. You're not only a liar. You're a dirty, slanderous, libellous, venomous villain and you ought to be horse-whipped. It's well known the world over – even in England – that Irish boys and girls are the chastest, purest, noblest, handsomest crowd of youngsters to be found wearing skirts or trousers. As for Irish motherhood, I wonder the pen didn't burn your fingers and the tongue turn black in your head at the things you said there a while back. Hasn't the Holy Father Himself said that the Irish Mother is an inspiration to the world –

CLEEVE: When did he say that?

ES: – with her devotion and her piety and her purity and her white hair and her black shawl and her red petticoat that is an heirloom for generations and her recipes for barm brack and griddle bread and soda cakes and bacon and cabbage. And she keeping hens, and turkeys for Christmas and fattening a piglet, and reading the letter from her son in Chicago with the tears running from under her iron-rimmed spectacles and dripping into the ashes of the hearth beside the big black iron kettle on the hob that does be drawing the strong wholesome black tea?

C: True for you, true for you! Did you know that in the old days the peasants in Connemara bought the best and most expensive teas that money could buy? The English bought tea dust, but the Irish farm wife would pay thirty shillings a pound for the best Darjeeling, and no tea merchant could fool her with less than the best. It was the Second World War and tea rationing that ruined all that. Half an ounce of tea a week, and people scraping carrots and drying the scrapings to eke out the tea, and gathering hips and haws and herbs from the hedgerows to give them the illusion of the real thing. In those six years the taste and knowledge of real tea was lost and now, yerrah, there isn't a woman in Ireland knows what tea is. Muck they buy. Pure muck. You used to be able to trot a mouse on a real mug of country tea. The little creature could dance on the surface without wetting its paws.

ES: Don't try and change the subject. You've slandered, libelled, blasphemed Irish motherhood, Irish womanhood, Irish manhood, Irish boyhood. Homosexuality forsooth! Where is the boy in Ireland knows the meaning of the word?

C: At Gay Rights headquarters?

ES: I won't allow it! I won't listen! You should be locked up. Is nothing sacred to you? What will the English think if they're fools enough to read your blasphemous drivel?

C: They'll think we're like them.

ES: We're not like them! We're Catholics. Irish Catholics. Gaelic speakers. Celts. The oldest culture in Europe, driven from our rightful heritage by ruthless barbarians, by the perfidious English. Oppressed, cruelly tortured, starved, beaten through seven centuries of wretchedness, we yet rose up again and again in our righteous anger to drive the invaders into the sea. And at last we triumphed! Our wills, our national consciousness steeled and tempered by the fires of the Easter Rising, the right rose tree of our liberty and nationhood wetted by the blood of our blessed martyrs, we rose a last time to tread the dastards underfoot, to sweep them away from Irish soil for ever, to lay claim to our own four green fields for ever and a day, and create on them a shining monument that is the wonder of the world – a monument built of the saintly bones of our blessed and courageous dead, our saintly mothers, our valiant boys, our tender maidens. The voices of our ancestral paradise in a paean of glorious victory –

C: Partition?

ES: Partition will be swept away! Not by violence but by the will of the people. Brother will clasp the hand of brother –

C: And Paisley will become Taoiseach. Those people are cleverer than we are. They work harder. They get up earlier. They're as cunning as foxes. It'd be a disaster for us if Partition ended.

ES: That does it! That finally does it! Is there a man or woman or talking child in this state that doesn't know that the whole ambition of every Irish man and woman is to end Partition? That that is the declared aim of every politician? Even 'the Other Crowd'? That our Leader is working ceaselessly day and night to end Partition? Our ministers? Our TDs [Irish MPs]? Our city councillors? Our county councillors? Our hierarchy? Our ambassadors abroad? Our representatives in the United Nations? Our members of the European Parliament? – and don't you dare mention their salaries. Nor their travel allowances. Nor their pensions. Selfless men and women. Wearing their hearts out with ceaseless toil. Not a thought for anything but ending Partition.

C: In 1926 when the Boundary Commission –

ES: I'm not going to listen. I'm warning you –

C: They could have changed the whole thing. The English expected it. Only the Southern members of the Commission didn't bother. They just left everything as it was – the provisional border that someone drew on a map in 1921. The English were astonished. No one knows to this day why it happened.

ES: It's a filthy lie! There's not an Irishman dead or alive who wouldn't give his heart's blood to end Partition! Our lost green fields!

Our separated brothers! And sisters! Our co-religionists!

C: We couldn't afford them if they came to join us of their own free will. And they don't want to join us.

ES: How can you say that and not drop dead at your own feet? Blasphemer, heretic, seaneen, West Brit, souper. Were you ever at Croke Park singing 'Erin go brach' while the teams came out to play the All Ireland championships? No. A day like that you'd be skulking at home watching the BBC and *Match of the Day* or *This Is Your Life*. Did you ever feel your back breaking and you with a loy in your hands getting in the turf against the long winter nights, and the wind whistling across the bog and the curlews crying? Were you ever out in a currach seeking the silver harvest of the deep in the strong Atlantic breakers, the Blaskets there behind you like whalebacks in the gloaming and nothing but a pocketful of cold potatoes to allay your hunger from golden dawn to crimson nightfall, and the porpoises playing about you like fairy people and a great whale threatening you with the terror of his jaws and the wind rising and the sky darkening? Were you ever out with the boys in '21 and the Tans hunting you and you with one rusty revolver and two Mills grenades between the six of you to set an ambush, and nothing but the courage of your hearts to keep you from flying for your lives when you heard the Tan lorries coming and the Auxiliaries in an armoured car sweeping the road in front? Did you ever do any of those things?

C: I went sailing in Dun Laoghaire harbour once –

ES: Did any of your ancestors ever sail in the coffin ships to Amerikay, all their possessions in a wee bundle wrapped up in an old petticoat and tears in their eyes and a lump in their throats as they saw the spire of Cobh cathedral fade in the dear distance and the lovely shore of Erin vanish for ever in the mists of the horizon?

C: No. But –

ES: Were any of your ancestors ever evicted out of their poor mud cabin by the heartless jeering redcoats and the landlord's bailiff, to weep by the roadside of a winter's day, the children crying, and the sticks of furniture smashed to pieces, and not a sack of potatoes between them and starvation?

C: I don't think so, but –

ES: Don't give me any more buts! There are no buts about being Irish! A man whose great-great-grandfather wasn't out in '98 is not an Irishman. Or his great-great-great-great-grandfather at the Yellow Ford. Or his own dear daddy or granddaddy in the GPO in '16.

C: I could tell you a joke about that – about all the people claiming pensions for being in the Post Office that Easter and someone working out that –

ES: That's enough! More than enough! There's things even a scoundrel like you couldn't bring yourself to say. Go home and hide your shame. Irish? You're no more Irish than one of those dirty Sunday newspapers that people like you do be reading in bed of a Sunday morning instead of going to Mass to ask God to forgive them for their sins. Get away from me! I'm ashamed to be in the same book with you.

C: I didn't want to start any of this. I only wanted to talk about the position of women. I thought you'd be pleased.

ES: Pleased? On their backs? Ruining their sons? Inviting boys home for the night? Is it the Devil is in you or what? Go and wash out your mouth with soap.)

There is no pleasing her about the position of Irishwomen, or about anything else. But if the status of women in Ireland is still far short of what it should be, it has improved a great deal over the past twenty years. One substantial improvement was achieved by the Succession Act of 1965, by which it was made virtually impossible for curmudgeonly old husbands to dispossess their wives in their wills, leaving everything to their mistress, or a nephew, or a cats' home, or the Church. All too often, the Church. Horrendous stories are told of legacies to the Church which left deserving relatives of the dead penniless and in dire need. And of the Church turning a deaf ear to pleas for natural justice to be done. Such things are no longer possible. A widow is entitled to between a third and half of her late husband's estate according to particular circumstances, and in her husband's lifetime as well as after his death she has rights in the matrimonial home that cannot be set aside without her willing consent.

Aside from such legal improvements, the general atmosphere of society has advanced out of the 19th century as well. As I said, it has become usual and natural for young women to have their own bank accounts – although all too often wives do not, remaining dependent on their husband's goodwill for every penny beyond the housekeeping. So that – again all too often – wives regard it as a duty to get 'every penny out of the old man' that they possibly can, needed or not. (Equally, Irishmen are often reluctant to make wills or take out life insurance, regarding it as 'morbid' – a failure which can leave a young widow even unhappier than she need have been.)

And as I said too, women drive cars – often, in the country, for the initial reason that the husband has lost his licence – and not many men make jokes any more about women drivers. Again, in the country particularly, women handle the daily finances, and a workman doing repairs to the house or a painting job will expect to deal 'with herself' rather than with the man of the house, and will resign himself to a tougher bargain in consequence.

It is necessary to make this distinction between town and country practices because in Ireland there is still a very definite division between the two. And this urban rural rift applies to many things besides wives' having partial control of money matters. (And even in the country this control is still not universal.) But the rift is not so much Irish as antique. In England, the countryside has been so deeply penetrated by city people, whether as commuters, week-enders, or retired couples, or escapers from the rat-race, that the distinction between town-dweller and countryman has been largely blurred.

Not much of this has yet happened in Ireland. Of course people from Dublin or Cork travel to Irish villages for business, or spend holidays in them, or have relatives who are still part of them. But there remains a sharp division between those who are city born and bred and those who are country born and bred. And not only a division but a hostile one. Under the warm Irish smiles of welcome for the Dublin visitor to the Irish farmhouse there lies a 19th-century suspicion of city ways and morals, or lack of them. While Dubliners have a deep contempt and hostility towards country people who come crowding into their city looking for jobs and flats and hospital beds and anything else in short supply. Country people, according to Dubliners, are both ignorant and cunning – 'They'd buy and sell you.' (In this latter category Cork people are worse than country people in Dubliners' eyes.) Country people are clannish – 'They'd never *really* let you in.' (Mayomen, Connemaramen, and Kerrymen, are reputed to be the worst of all in this regard, in that order. Although some Dublin experts would rate Kerrymen as even worse than Mayomen. People from County Cork – as opposed to Cork City – are thought to be merely thick.)

Country girls are not only thick in mind. They are also thick in body, according to Dublin legend – 'Beef to the heels, like a Mullingar heifer.' Or else both ferocious and treacherous – mountain women in particular. And ignorant as an ass in a ditch – 'They'd keep coals in the bath and wash their feet in the WC. If they ever did wash their feet.'

But all these are legends and libels of yesterday rather than today, lingering on as unkind jokes rather than as real beliefs. But as jokes they do still colour beliefs, and the clannishness and suspicion are still real enough – as they are in England, even after thirty years of *The Archers.*

There is also the survival in the country of the Victorian patriarch, again a 19th-century rather than an Irish phenomenon. He is the elderly farmer clinging to authority over aged wife and middle-aged sons and daughters, long after reason suggests that he should have retired. He uses his Last Will and Testament as a whip to keep them obedient, and bitterly resents the restrictions placed on him by the Succession Act, that obliges him to some sort of fairness. He tries to prevent sons marrying and daughters leaving. He treats his wife as a slave.

But again, and mercifully, his is a disappearing breed. Television has taught the remotest farm folk that another way of life exists, even for women. And, as has been said, there is another type of farmer who not only allows but expects his wife to handle a great deal of the farm expenditure, or at least that part of it that applies to the farmhouse. Country wives in Ireland are not all slaves, just as many city wives are far from liberated.

There have been changes for the better for women in a hundred directions over the last twenty years. More girls go to university, and more take up careers rather than mere jobs when they leave school or college. There are women doctors, lawyers, solicitors, journalists, TV announcers (although none in really influential positions). There are women fighting for women's rights. There are all the signs of women's self-conscious self-assertion that there are in England, and one can see evidence of this even in the way women walk and hold themselves. Twenty and thirty years ago girls tended to stoop their shoulders, as if they were ashamed of having breasts, and also as if they had never had physical training. Today they hold themselves as well as any women anywhere.

Yet there is still nothing like real equality, legal or social, between Irish men and Irish women. It's a man's country, run according to male traditions, and a great many women accept this as if it was a law of nature or the Will of God, rather than a masculine confidence trick. They resign themselves to it or, as I have said, even reinforce it by bringing up their sons to exploit it.

If not the Will of God, is it the Will of the Church that this should be so? The Church, in spite of the Virgin Mary and several hundred thousand nuns, is a masculine organisation, which has always regarded women's role as inferior – 'Women, be subject to your husbands.' And to your priests, in a way that men are *not* subject to priests. No priest in confession talks to a man the way he talks to a woman. In the one case he persuades, in the other he orders. Husbands have rights over wives' bodies, but wives have no rights over husbands' bodies.

Which reminds me of another startlingly visible physical inequality between Irish men and Irish women. Women are expected to look attractive, to keep themselves in fine physical trim, smartly dressed, well made-up, hair charming, eyes bright with health. If they don't, they're dead. Every advertisement, TV commercial, soap opera, magazine article, and their boy-friends, tell them this. This may seem in flat contradiction of the earlier statement that Irish men often choose plain wives and leave beautiful girls on the shelf, and so they do, all too often. But if the beautiful girl is to have any hope of getting off the shelf she has to keep herself as smart as paint, and even the plain girls are expected to be clean and neat and well turned-out.

But no one tells the young men the equivalent. Men do not have to look attractive. The assumption is that, being men, they *are* attractive, simply by that fact of masculinity. If they clean their teeth and shave daily that's all that any woman can expect of them. Beer bellies, sagging chests, spindle legs, acne, premature baldness – no matter – they are *males*, irresistible to women, God's chosen sex.

And the sex that God chose to run His Church. Yet by a paradox that is certainly not simply Irish, but universal throughout all Catholic countries, women are not only the chief victims of the Church, made to realise from their earliest years that they are of the race of Eve and the occasion of the Fall – they are also the Church's chief supporters. Every country curate knows the terror of the half-dozen pious matrons of the parish, who oversee its morality with more gimlet-eyed ferocity than the most Jansenist parish priest could exercise. Women are the fund-raisers of the Church. Women are the Mass-goers; they see that their children go to Mass, and, if possible, see that their husbands go to Mass as well. (Men go to Mass as a duty, women go as a recreation.) Women look after the parish clergy and see that they have clean socks and new vestments. Women clean the churches and do the flowers. If women stopped doing these things the Church would disintegrate within ten years. Less. And if women wanted to exercise the power they possess in the Church there would not only be women priests, there would be a woman Pope.

But women do not want to exercise that power, in Ireland or elsewhere, any more than they want to exercise their voting power in politics. Why not is a mystery, but that they do not is a fact.

(An Irish woman of great piety and penetrating common sense remarked indignantly on reading this passage that Irishwomen do *not* see to priests' having clean socks. In a limited, literal sense this may be true, because the priest's housekeeper is a vanishing breed. Priests often have to cook their own breakfasts and see to their own domestic affairs like other bachelors. But among the only very few priests I know personally there is at least one who has solved part of this problem by bringing his laundry to a woman friend every week. There is not a pick of harm in the friendship, and not a reason in the world why the poor man shouldn't get his laundry done for him if he can manage it. But it is still a woman who does it for him.)

6 Drink

The Irish have always had a reputation for drinking too much, and over the years they have done their best to deserve it, not only at home, but everywhere they have gone. The 'drunken Irishman' is as firmly outlined a stereotype as exists in world mythology. In New York surveys have consistently shown the ethnic Irish at the top of the drinking table, with ethnic Jews at the bottom.

Is this nurture or nature? The Jews and the Catholic Irish share similarly powerful religious backgrounds, and both races have a tradition of influential mother figures. So, if it is not nurture, is it nature? Race? Celtic blood? The Romans remarked on the Celtic love of hard liquor. Is this, at last, a true Celtic trait, a significant if inglorious distinction and real difference betweel Gael and Gall? Irish and Sassenach? Us and you? Perhaps, but if it is, one cannot rely on Roman evidence. When they could afford it Romans drank enormously themselves, and when they came in contact with the Germanic tribes, including the Saxons, they remarked on how much they drank, as well. According to Saxon accounts, the Saxon warrior class drank itself insensible every night, as a matter of course. And here and there in ancient literature one comes across suggestions that when Celt and Saxon were in fiercest conflict, during the Dark Ages, the Celts despised the Saxons as brutish sots.

(Incidentally, the Jews were clearly not always a sober community. When Samuel's mother went to the temple to pray to Yahweh to give her a son, the High Priest 'was watching her mouth, for she was speaking under her breath; her lips were moving but her voice could not be heard. He therefore supposed that she was drunk ... ' Which suggests that this was a fairly common condition, even for women, and even in the temple. And both Isaiah and Amos condemn excessive drinking among the Jewish upper and priestly classes, even 'by the side of every altar' where they 'drink the wine of the people they have fined in the house of their God ... ')

The historical Irish excuse for the heavy consumption of whiskey (*Uisce beatha*, the water of life, exact equivalent of *eau de vie*) is the climate. A man who had spent a wet day in wet clothes on a sodden bog, whether shooting snipe, or redcoats, or landlords, needed a nip or two when he at last reached shelter (the traditional nip was the contents of a half egg shell.)

There must be something in this kindly medical theory, because all the invaders of Ireland have taken to the bottle like swans to the surface of an inviting lake. Jonah Barrington, lawyer, judge, Ascendancy scapegrace of impeccably Protestant English ancestry, although of a family long-established in Ireland, describes in his memoirs the murderous drinking parties of apple punch in his grandfather's day. Cart-loads of roasted apples soaked in barrelfuls of brandy were set out before the house party – the gentry and half gentry from the neighbourhood being all invited – and for ten days on end there were nothing but drunken shouts of glee, punctuated by shrieks of pain from the gout-ridden as the brandy reached their inflamed toes. By the end of ten days the lustiest drinkers of all were beginning to fade, and the weaklings were already stretched under tables, in beds, under beds, on piles of straw in the stables, or being trundled home on wheelbarrows or in carts by their peasant retainers. But it may need to be repeated that this was a Protestant shindig, an English, Sassenach celebration of the good things of life, while the Catholic serfs looked on in Celtic jealousy and admiration.

(Although it has nothing to do with drink, another of Barrington's stories deserves telling here. One of his female ancestors at the beginning of the 18th century was a proud and handsome woman, much loved by her Catholic servants. One day a half-mounted gentlemen – a kind of Irish yeoman class – insulted her, and the next morning at breakfast, still burning with noble indignation, she recited the story in front of her butler, and finished it by crying 'I'd like to have the rascal's ears!'

At dinner that night they were presented to her, in a covered silver dish.)

But back to whiskey (an Irish invention, purloined and emasculated by the Scotch). Do the Irish today drink all that much? Do they really drink more than you do? Those with an interest in finding a flattering answer say 'No', as one might expect. The distillers, the bar owners, the government – who would be in a sad state for ready cash if the whole population stopped drinking – all agree with piously uplifted hands that *some* Irishmen drink too much (and even some women of latter years), but that the problem is not nearly as bad as critics make out.

The critics, on the contrary, claim that we have one of the worst records in Europe for alcoholism and alcohol-related illnesses and legal offences. Both sides back their arguments with statistics, and several factors make the statistics apparently capable of supporting either side, according to your preference. First and foremost, the statistics fail to make clear how many Irish men and women are involved in drinking the total volume of liquor consumed in the South. There are just over 3,443,000 people in Southern Ireland, and if one divides the total Irish consumption of alcohol by that figure, the resulting national *per capita* consumption is not all that alarming, though it does place Ireland at the top of Europe's beer-drinking league (but only fourth in spirits and bottom in wine).

But if one then cuts out of the calculation all those who do not drink through age or choice, the picture changes. Babies do not drink, or not much. And young people under sixteen don't drink much because they are not allowed to, and adolescents under eighteen are not supposed to. (Though what does a barman do when a sixteen-year-old skinhead in bovver boots, chains and riot gear says he wants a glass of shandy?) This accounts for over a third of the population. Then there are at least 150,000 Pioneers, that is, sworn Total Abstainers. And if one takes into account such groups as nuns, the very old, hospital and mental long-term patients, and abstainers who do not belong to the Pioneers, one can reckon that roughly half the population drinks no alcohol at all.

This immediately doubles the real *per capita* consumption given in the statistics. And if one goes on to consider that in general women drink very much less than men – although some women are trying very hard to catch up, just as some children are, the figures for female and child alcoholism being already alarming – but if one accepts the generalisation that the really serious drinking in the Republic is done by men, aided heroically by a few women and children, then the figures change again. The vast proportion of Ireland's drinking is done by a fraction of the population. To put it at its most charitable, the total figures for beer and spirits should be divided not by almost $3\frac{1}{2}$ million, but by at most 1 million drinkers, to obtain a picture of what a real Irish drinker consumes every year, or every day.

The beer figures for 1981, according to Messrs Arthur Guinness's statistical department, were 2,681,000 barrels of beers, including stout, each barrel containing 36 gallons, making a total of 114,516,000 gallons, or 916,128,000 pints. This means that if the estimate of 1 million beer drinkers in Ireland is correct, then each of them consumed 916 pints during the year, or between 17 or 18 pints a week. Which represents a modest $2\frac{1}{2}$ pints per night, every night of the year, at just over £1 a pint. (Messrs Guinness regard, unofficially, $1\frac{1}{2}$ pints a night as representing a 'serious' interest in beer or stout. Really serious drinkers will smile indulgently at the 'shock-horror' tone of the above figures. 'Two and a half pints a night? Get out of that. I can put away seven or eight and not feel the difference.')

Not many people, and still fewer official spokesmen, want to admit what this kind of consumption does to Ireland's general state of health. The government makes too much out of taxes on alcohol to underline the effects on those who drink a lot of it. And unofficial spokespersons who do so are accused variously of being killjoys, or of damaging Ireland's reputation (Heavens above! As far as alcohol is concerned, what reputation?), or simply of lying for their own devious purposes. At the least hint that the government might take steps, by higher taxes or health warnings, to curb consumption, the drink lobby, from distillers to the Barmen's Union, cries blue murder. Jobs will be lost. Prosperity will be lost. Pubs will close. Brewers will go bankrupt. (One has, recently, to the sorrow of many who admired the smooth quality of its product. But it was not lack of hearty drinkers that temporarily closed its doors.)

One indication of the amount of damage done is provided by Alcoholics Anonymous. The membership – all of reformed alcoholics – is only 5,000. But the Association's well informed estimate is that its membership represents only 7 per cent of the total number of practising alcoholics in the country, which gives a figure of just over 70,000. Or about 1 in 14 of the before-mentioned 1 million serious drinkers.

One can juggle these figures in almost any way that one likes, to make them seem more or less impressive. But 70,000 alcoholics out of a population of less than $3\frac{1}{2}$ millions is a lot of alcoholics. Added to which, a great many drinkers damage themselves, their families, their employment and the general economy without ever becoming alcholics, simply by always functioning well below par.

Add to that sort of damage all the drink-related illnesses, hospital beds occupied, nurses and doctors occupied, motor accidents and crimes caused by drink, and you have a problem that outweighs a great many more publicised problems, such as whether teenagers should have access to contraceptives.

As a footnote to these figures one can consider the matter of blood and urine samples taken from drivers by the Guards. During the three months, April, May, June, 1982, 2,132 drivers (88 per cent of those tested) were found to have more than 100 milligrams of alcohol per 100 millilitres of blood (already a generous allowance by the standards of some other countries, where for a driver to have 80 or even 50 milligrams per 100 millilitres constitutes an offence.) But 676 of those tested had over 200 milligrams, twice even the Irish limit, and around 170 had 250 milligrams of alcohol per 100 millilitres of blood. How dangerous that made them I leave to your imagination, but wise drivers avoid driving in Ireland in the half hour or so following public-house closing times.

And lest anyone think that I am making a mountain out of an alcoholic molehill, let me cite two reports which appeared in the *Irish Times* in September 1982. On the 23rd the Medico-Social Research Board was quoted by Dr David Nowlan as saying in its report for 1981 that 'psychiatric hospital admissions for alcoholism are still much higher in Ireland than in England and are particularly high for alcoholism and alcoholic psychosis'. Among Irish people living in England the 'number of admissions for ... alcohol related diagnoses' were five times as great for Irish immigrants as they were for the English. The one point in this sad report that could give any comfort to a Southern Irishman is that the Northern Irish seem even worse. Immigrants from Northern Ireland in England have an alcohol-related admission rate to psychiatric hospitals seven times that of the native English. Even so, these horrifying figures are better than they are for the Irish who stayed at home.

Just two weeks earlier, again in the *Irish Times*, Dick Hogan had reported on the Simon Community in Cork. He painted a vivid picture of what the bare statistics really mean in human suffering, waste and indignity:

In the past year, 41 regular residents of the Simon Community in Cork were imprisoned for public drunkenness at a cost to the State of £63,000.

The Simon administrator in the city, Ms Glen Spray, said yesterday that if the money had been given instead to the Simon Community, it would have been able to ensure that at least some of those imprisoned received help for their problems.

Ms Spray, who was presenting the community's annual report, said that vast amounts of State funds were being squandered on locking away people with problems who would eventually return to society with the same problems.

In the past year, she said, the Simon Community budget in Cork totalled £86,000 of which £12,000 was made available by the Southern Health Board.

'The remainder of the money we begged or got from people who made voluntary donations. But our biggest problem is that from year to year, we do not know if the money will be there or not ... It is now recognised that the kind of care needed for these people centres around the provision of community-based specialised hostels for alcoholics and detoxification facilities. We have none in Cork.

'Ironically, for many, prison is the only place available where they have a bed for the night, food and a brief chance to dry out. But what chance is that when they are thrown back onto the streets with nowhere to go and no one to bother until they appear back in court.

'It is amazing that we are prepared to spend £51,600 per year to keep one child in Loughan House, the only children's prison in Europe. We will spend another £20 million on a proposed prison for women in Clondalkin. We are continually pouring public money down the drain by locking up people who need medical treatment and a home to go to.'

According to the Simon Community, the problem of homeless children is growing in Cork and will continue to do so. Last year the community met 10 unattached children, one a 14-year-old girl who was already a heavy drinker and who had become a prostitute. 'The plight of this young girl was publicised by us a year ago. The only difference now is that there are four other children hanging around with her.'

A few weeks later the *Evening Press* quoted Fr James Healy, professor of Moral Theology at the Milltown Institute in Dublin, as saying that between 300 and 600 Irish priests (out of the total of 3,797 diocesan and 2,209 Order priests) have 'alcohol-related problems'. Fr Healy compares this to the Church in the United States, where 10,000 nuns and 5,000 priests are in the same unhappy situation. 'In Ireland,' added Fr Healy, 'the problem is proportionately the same among priests,' although not, so far, among nuns. It would be interesting to know if in the USA priests of Irish descent have a greater tendency to alcoholism than other priests.

Among several friends of mine who drank more than they should there was one who rather than being described as a professional man with a drinking problem, might better have been described as a drinking man with a professional problem. Over the years he drank his way through a substantial estate. He never did any practical work, having a lively dislike of his profession, as well as a sincere incapacity for it. His wife was reduced to selling the furniture. But whatever else suffered, he always found money for drink, and the bailiffs never moved in. The bank always gave him credit. The shops always gave him credit. Things never got really tough until he gave up drinking. Then the creditors pounced and everything had to be sold. But he still never did any work. And he has never starved, mainly thanks to a devoted and inestimable wife. God looks after heavy drinkers.

Another friend of mine (why *shouldn't* I be personal? Would it add a sense of dignity and veracity if I was to say a Mr A?) – another friend of mine who drank enormously (two bottles of whiskey a day in his prime) was a fine painter when he was sober enough to hold a brush. But he much preferred whiskey to art. (He was once 'cured' of whiskey by aversion therapy. The cure worked very well, but unfortunately only for whiskey. He started drinking gin instead, which he didn't much like. However, after a while the aversion wore off and he was happy again.)

In a town and time of notoriously heavy drinkers he was notoriously notorious. He weighed seventeen stone, which made him difficult to miss when he was drunk, and difficult to deal with when he was argumentative. He was banned from almost every public house in Dublin and often had to do his drinking at home, in an attic studio in St Stephen's Green, with the wind whistling through the skylight and ghosts on the staircase. More than once he tottered downstairs to collect milk from the doorstep and managed to lock himself out stark naked. A passing Guard would wrap him in a Garda raincoat and call the fire brigade to get him back in again. Once, when no Guard was available a small passer-by lent him a rather small mackintosh and he rang me from a nearby hotel to come and rescue him. I found him at the bar looking like a porpoise in a waterproof waistcoat, and he begged me to go drinking with him for the rest of the morning. He was very upset when I wouldn't.

He had a complexly affectionate relationship with the Gardai, who were frequently obliged to arrest him for causing disturbances. When the Civic Guards first recruited women (known as Ban Gardai) my friend saw a small Ban Garda patrolling self-consciously down Grafton Street in her smart new uniform and, swooping on her, he draped his seventeen-stone around her and shouted 'Kiss me!', which sounds delightfully (or reprehensibly) silly. But there was a degree of malice in it, because he was not, on the whole, fond of women as a class. He liked pretty and sympathetic examples, but not the genus. He was also intensely moral, or moralistic. In one pub he was still allowed into there was a female customer he knew very well, but wouldn't speak to, because she was 'immoral'. When my wife, who had been at school with this woman said 'Hallo' to her in his presence our friend was furious, asking her did she not know what the woman *was*?

When he was drunk he could be delightful, if difficult, company, full of good stories. When he was sober he was painfully shy and almost mute, which offers a fragment of explanation as to why so many Irishmen drink so much. They feel so inadequate when they are sober. (As the psychiatrist said to his patient, it's no wonder you have an inferiority complex, you *are* inferior.)

One might have supposed – the unco' guid would no doubt like to suppose – that so much drinking must have shattered his health. It did no such thing. He had a fine head of pitch-black hair into his sixties, and whatever state his liver was in it never seemed to bother him. One day he died suddenly and peacefully, in a monastery where he had secured a commission to paint a mural, surrounded by the monks and by the consolations of religion. I believe he was very drunk at the time, although no doubt some hagiographer will claim he was sober. I don't think one should wish that to be true, because when he was sober he was terrified of the dark.

If anyone who loved him recognises this thumbnail sketch, I hope they will not be offended, for no offence is intended. I loved him too, and my wife did one of the few practical things that was ever done for him, by having part of his studio (as bleak and cold an attic as ever existed) done up as a bed-sitting-room, with a studio couch, and carpets, and curtains, and an electric fire. When it was done he sat staring at everything, crying, and saying 'Look at the carpet!' and pulling the curtains back and forth. (Another time, when he was in bed with 'flu, the curate* from a local pub came up to collect a long-standing debt for drinks on the slate. My friend pulled the blankets over his head and shouted 'I'm not here'. In a sense he wasn't.)

His ambition in life was to have a job with a salary, and he could never understand why no one would give him one. He appealed to old friends in the government to recommend him for some official position, such as curator of the National Gallery, and was deeply

* Barman, bar-owner's assistant.

resentful when they failed to keep their promises. He was like a sixty-year-old child, an enormous, difficult – and endlessly selfish – child, and it may be impossible for any non-Irish reader to understand why people tolerated him, let alone loved him, but a great many people did, and remember him to this day with tears of affection.

This long story has been worth dwelling on because it illustrates several peculiarities of Irish society. First and above all, the enormous toleration in Ireland for drunks. No matter what a man does (women are a different case here, as in so much else in Ireland), if he was drunk when he did it he runs a fair chance of being excused. Murder will be regarded as manslaughter – or even disregarded, as the social worker's report quoted earlier suggests. A hit-and-run driver will plead drink if he is caught, and the plea is likely to be accepted in mitigation of the offence (this is changing, but far too slowly). This toleration holds true all the way through society. A man in State or semi-State employment who is known to his employers to be an alcoholic will be given every possible help to disguise his affliction – 'sick' leave, a blind eye to absences, tolerance of inefficiency, not just once or twice, or for a period, but for a lifetime. Bank managers, solicitors, doctors, politicians – if they drink too much they can almost always count on a sympathetic and endlessly tolerant cover-up for their misdemeanours.

And one is tempted to say 'How Irish! How *Celtic*! How charmingly *local*!' (Or disgustingly so, as the fancy takes you.) But is it? Do the English not have problem drinkers in responsible positions? Who are supported and covered-up for by their friends, far beyond the limits of real friendship and reason? The memoirs of leading English politicians and socialites suggest that the English are just as affected by this as the Irish. So are the Americans. So are the French. (And some elderly French politicians chase twelve-year-old girls as well, which is not a widespread habit in Dáil Eireann.)

Another factor in the painter's story which might more truly be called Irish, rather than universal, is 'respect'. Respect for talent, however misused and abused. He was penniless, often disgusting, but talented. And people who may well have shuddered at the drunkenness or condemned it or lamented it, respected the talent. This included the Guards who arrested him and the Justices who fined him – or let him off with a caution. Moreover, he was of 'good stock'. He was a drunk, but not a slob. Not a yahoo. He got drunk with style. This could not and cannot be said for the vast majority of Irish drunks, who simply get nastier the more they drink, and often violent along with it. There is nothing funny about being drunk, or excusable, and one of our worst social faults in Ireland is that all too often we *do* find it funny, and do excuse it. And we forget about the misery the man is causing to his own family, and the cost to society of putting up with his imbecility.

I say he and his. Women are beginning to catch up, as the statistics for alcoholism among women show. So, tragically, are children. A friend reading these pages made the following comments:

> You say 'young people under sixteen don't drink much because they are not allowed to'. The fact is, they do. (I think the supermarkets are to blame, too.) 12-, 13-, 14-, 15-, and 16-year-olds *do* drink. Some say it's as much a problem for those age groups as drugs. And as for serving under-age drinkers, the barman has even a greater problem with girls (who *do* drink under age). My son was rather horrified, in a local pub that is notorious for serving drink to under-age teenagers, to find a 14-year-old girl there, someone's sister, and the 14-year-old was so made up etc that she could easily have been taken for 18. Local pressure from parents had this publican's licence taken away from him, but he can in law have it passed on to some other member of his family (I don't know what the legal process is. Maybe they apply afresh and can't be refused). Anyway, he managed to have it transferred first to his wife, then to his son and as he has several daughters it seems likely to go on and on. He is doing so well that he has built an extension at the back, and youngsters come to there from all over the city. They got so rowdy on Saturday nights that for a while the busmen refused to come right into the village and stopped the bus a few stops before the terminus.

A new twist to the 'Irish drunk' story is provided by present-day smuggling across the Border. Drink prices in the Republic, because of increased taxes, have risen to a point where a bottle of spirits costs twice as much south of the Border as it does in the North. Not unnaturally people in the South have begun to cast envious eyes northwards, and any one living near enough and with transport available has been tempted to slip across the Border for his nightly quota, rather than stay at home and feed the tax man. Coach parties are organised to travel north from as far south as Cork, returning in high good humour with enough liquor and other treasures to repay the cost of their journey twice over. Or they take day trips to Holyhead. Or they go into the business on a grander scale, slipping over the Border and back at unguarded crossing points and bringing enough whiskey in their car boots, or in borrowed vans, to give a village a cut-price hangover. Publicans south of the Border view this traffic – and the empty bars – with less than pleased expressions. So far into fiscal 1983 it is reckoned that the Southern exchequer has lost £40 to £45 million in taxes because of the fall off in Southern drink sales. This will be reflected in the teetotal statistics as a welcome access of sobriety. But the statistics will be wrong.

7 Literature

As a restorative and corrective after these ugly controversies about religion and sex and drink, it is a pleasant duty to turn to the subject of Irish literature. Surely there can be no controversy here, only sweetness and light?

Unfortunately, even here, controversy begins with the first words spoken. What *is* Irish literature? Books written in Ireland? Books written by Irish men and women? In English as well as Irish? Or only in Irish? The strictest view, and really the only fully logical one, is that put forward by Daniel Corkery in *Synge and Anglo-Irish Literature*. He claimed that *all* so called Anglo-Irish literature was in reality merely Anglo, and no more Irish literature then Fenimore Cooper's *Leatherstocking Tales* are Red Indian literature. From Maria Edgeworth to Yeats and Shaw, the Anglo-Irish writers were colonial writers, writing as colonists for home consumption. Their points of view were English rather than Irish, their audience was in London rather than in Dublin. They might, as Miss Edgeworth did, and Yeats did, and a hundred others in between and before did, *sympathise* with the native Irish, but they were not *of* them. They might present to English readers what understanding they had of Irish problems, but it was an English-educated, English-oriented understanding, a colonialists' understanding, and no more genuinely Irish than Kipling's *Plain Tales from the Hills* is genuinely Indian. Good literature, perhaps, even very good literature. But not *Irish*.

With one exception, the only literature Corkery would accept as Irish, blood and bone and flesh Irish, was that written *in* Irish, by writers born and brought up speaking Irish, singing and breathing Irish from the cradle, their minds shaped by Irish legends and Irish poetry and Irish tales, by the Irish rivers and the Irish hills, and by Irish history.

It is a stark but arguable and logical doctrine. Or it is until Corkery drives a coach-and-pair through it by making an exception for the Anglo-Irish playwright John Millington Synge, because, Corkery held, he was the one English-speaking writer so to catch the tones and rhythms and speech and thoughts and quirks of Gaelic, peasant Ireland as in effect to become truly Irish himself.

Synge was a wonderful playwright to be sure, but if you make an exception of him, why not of Lady Gregory (who was a better playwright than some now allow, and who also, despite the jeers at her 'Kiltartan' dialogue, caught the genuine tones of the peasantry)? And of Yeats? And of Lady Morgan (much less a figure of fun than Corkery might have held her to be if he troubled to remember her), who was the daughter of a native Irish-speaker and who herself spoke Irish? (She was also one of the first to collect and save native Irish songs before they vanished forever.)

But there remains, none the less, a persuasiveness about Corkery's argument. Is Goldsmith really an *Irish* writer? 'The Deserted Village' was based on a village in Ireland, as the text occasionally betrays, but to secure an English readership (the only one that could keep him from starving to death) Goldsmith transposed the whole thing to an English setting, and in doing so deprived it of half of its historical and social value.

Is Shaw *really* an Irish playwright? *St Joan? Major Barbara? the Apple Cart?* What did he ever write except *John Bull's Other Island* that had *anything* Irish about it? His wit? Shaw grew up in Dublin and one could argue very strongly that Dublin is not an Irish city, but an English provincial one – indeed, a number of people in Ireland *do* argue this. Or Oscar Wilde? Oscar's mother had a deep interest in Irish legends and mythology (she made and published a fine collection of folktales, *Ancient Legends of Ireland*, and she may have passed on this interest to her son, but there is no sign of it in his work). Oscar Wilde needs to be lumped in with the long list of emigrants who sold whatever was Irish in their birthright for a good living in England.

Why not? Why shouldn't they? Who would have given poor Thomas Moore the time of day in Ireland? If Wilde had stayed in Dublin he might as well have become a dentist, if Sheridan had stayed he wouldn't have earned enough to become bankrupt. But to say these things is not to alter the fact. It is very hard to regard *The Rivals* or Tom Moore's drawing-room ditties (*Irish Melodies, Lalla Rookh*, etc) as *Irish* literature.

One could as easily go from one extreme to the other, from ultra-exclusiveness and chauvinism to claiming every visitor to Ireland as 'Irish'. (Incidentally, do you know where the word 'chauvinism' comes from? You don't want to know? You do. You do. It comes from the name of an estimable and much-wounded French soldier of the First Empire, Monsieur Nicolas Chauvin, who so idolised Napoleon and *la Patrie* that he became a figure of fun even to his friends. Cogniard borrowed his name for a character in a popular stage show, *La Cocarde Tricolore* of 1831, and he features in several other French plays. You see? We Irish are cosmopolitans, filled with precious scraps of knowledge from the byways of history. Not for us the stodgy Sassenach insularity of our neighbours.)

(ES: Will you get back to the point? If there is a point?

C: There is. There is. I think.)

What was the point? Chauvinism? Literature? Tom Moore? Yes. One could as easily claim more, rather than less. Indulge in a vainglorious pan-Celticism, that would include, say, the Brontës in Irish literature. And Wilkie Collins. (I once read a persuasive pamphlet proving that Shakespeare was Irish.) After all, the Brontës' father was an Irishman, named Prunty – he thought Brontë sounded more respectable. (He also shot holes in the kitchen door at Haworth with his duelling pistols when he felt depressed, which seems to have been fairly often, or so it is said.) And not only was their father Irish, their mother was Cornish, which is the next best thing, and is certainly not English. Wilkie Collins's grandfather was born in Wicklow, and Congreve was educated in Kilkenny. George Borrow was partly educated in Clonmel, and claims even to have learned Irish there. Are they less 'Irish' than Maria Edgeworth, who never saw Ireland until she was fourteen? And is Samuel Beckett Irish? He lives in Paris and writes in French. (For that matter, is Simenon Belgian? For a long time he lived in America before moving to Switzerland, and *he* writes in French.)

Only recently, a hard-fought seminar took place in Dublin on the subject of Anglo-Irish literature, at which it was proposed – and rejected – that we should drop the word 'Anglo' altogether. So, as you can see, controversy is unavoidable.

(ES: Write about the scenery. Write about Killarney.

C: You mean the way the jarveys overcharge the tourists? And what it costs for dinner in the hotels? And the condition of the lakes? And that hotel they built in the Gap of Dunloe? And the German bungalows? And –

ES: All right, all right. Go back to literature. I'm going to tell Mr Haughey about this. He'll stop your exemption from income tax. I knew that was a terrible idea, letting writers off paying tax. You've all got ideas above your station. God be with the days when writers all starved in attics. Then they produced *real* literature. Not this modern filth only full of sex and violence. Mangan, James Mangan now. *There* was a poet for you. 'Dark Rosaleen'. 'The Spanish ships are on the sea –' Oh, *he* was a poet all right. He knew his place in Irish society. Dry bread and TB. *That's* what creates poetry, not hamburgers in McDonald's, and tax-free living and holidays on the Costa Brava. How can an Irish poet go to the Costa Brava and look himself in the face when he comes home? It's to the Aran Islands he should be going, on his own two feet, shod in pampooties, to freshen his soul at the pure fountain of the living language – the Costa Brava! Fish and chips! Davy Byrne's with a young wan drinking vodkas and tonics. Literature, how are ye?

C: It's true, it's true, it's all true. But –

ES: There are no buts. Feed a poet and destroy a poet. Blind Raftery now. *There* was a poet. Not even a roof to his head. Living in a ditch. No sight to his eyes, the poor creature. But a poet. The true voice of the Gael.

> *I am Raftery the poet,*
> *Full of hope and love,*
> *Going west on my journey*
> *By the light of my heart ...*

Oh, don't tell me about modern poets! Your Kinsellas and Montagues and Seamus Heaneys, driving about in motor cars and having bank accounts and winning prizes. The day TB was eradicated out of Ireland was the death-day of poetry. Go away with you and have masses said for Blind Raftery and James Mangan and Eoghan Rua and all the others, may the earth rest lightly on them and the sun of Heaven shine warm on them and God's mercy reward them.)

Amen. Amen. I would gladly spend all night telling you about Gaelic poets, if I knew enough. Unhappily I don't. But I will happily devote part of a day to literature written in English. (I still don't know enough, but it is easier to conceal ignorance of your own language.) Of the 'modern' writers, I would place Liam O'Flaherty top of my list, much as I admire Frank O'Connor and Sean O'Faolain. But what could I tell you about any of these that you don't already know? And what about the really modern writers, the young lions of today rather than yesterday?

Who, among the small multitude of novelists, poets, playwrights, essayists, travel writers and *enfants terribles* of letters now at work in Ireland, whether in English or in Irish, are the O'Connors, the Ó Faolains, the O'Flahertys, the Yeatses, the Shaws, the Wildes, the Kate O'Briens of future critical acclaim? And who am I to single them out?

Brendan Behan has already entered the pantheon, as much for his persona as for his writing. Edna O'Brien needs no additional help from me to achieve public notice. Molly Keane with *Good Behaviour*,* Maeve Binchy with *Light a Penny Candle*, have each written a best-seller. Dervla Murphy is highly regarded as a travel writer. Brian Friel and Hugh Leonard have made themselves reputations on Broadway and in the West End. Seamus Heaney, the Northern poet, has achieved cult status in America and, even more remarkable, has achieved critical acceptance and praise in both the North and South of Ireland. He is a familiar voice on the BBC.

Brian Moore and John Banville have each built solid, and to all appearances lasting, reputations with novels that the generality of critics respect, and that have also pleased the public. So has William

---

* A wonderful novel, essential reading, together with Somerville and Ross and Elizabeth Bowen, for anyone who wants to understand the Anglo-Irish.

Trevor. So has Ben Kiely. So has John Broderick.

But beyond that handful of uncontroversial names – uncontroversial in the sense that it is unlikely that anyone would disclaim them as honourably representing some facet of modern Irish writing in English – who else? Ireland teems with writers, in the way that Paris teems with painters (which reminds me, visual illiterate that I am, that in this whole gallifmaufry of a book I have said not one word about Irish painters, or sculptors, or for that matter musicians or composers, or actors, or designers, except to describe my drunken painter friend. *Mea culpa.* I am an ignorant, philistine man, who knows more about Dallas than about Dingle. Why have I allowed myself to write this book? My abject apologies to all concerned. I can only say that I am unfit to praise them.)

But the writers, the writers. I am unfit to praise them too, and still less to select them for inclusion here in this ephemeral gallery. An added problem is that below a certain majestic level of world renown, native readers rarely agree with foreigners as to which of their native writers is really worthy of praise. Taking English examples, the French thought Charles Morgan the finest of talents, an opinion not widely shared in England. The Russians hailed C.P. Snow as a master worthy of a Nobel Prize, while English critics regarded him as humdrum. On the other hand, German critics could never understand Shaw's reputation because his translations into German were so bad. With a Dubliner's perversity, Shaw selected a good Socialist as his translator, rather than a competent linguist.

Turning back to Irish writers, even among the names I have mentioned, one or two will cause the sterner Irish critics to grind their teeth. Indeed, some of them have already ground their teeth at one another, without need of a prompt from me, while names which ring like golden bells to Irish critical ears have often failed to impress English or American critics, or even publishers. It might be invidious, and certainly dangerous, to say which, but there are certainly some very fine Irish writers who have received less than what our critics consider to be their due abroad. John B. Keane the playwright and author of many books of letters – a genre almost unknown in England except for C.S. Lewis's *Screwtape Letters* – is before all else a country writer, and even in Ireland the critics – who tend to be Dubliners – have been close-fisted in their praise. Because, one feels, he *is* a country writer. The same talent displayed by a Dublin writer would surely have made him the critics' darling. But there is also the fact that he is a full-blooded writer; he enjoys melodrama, and Dublin critics, like city-based critics elsewhere, seem to prefer books and plays in which there is no drama of any kind. But if a stranger was looking for one modern writer who would introduce him or her to the realities of modern Ireland, told with humour, irony and passion, then the first name I would offer would be Keane's.

Francis Stuart is another writer less considered abroad than at home. Here he is the *éminence grise* of Irish letters, but abroad he is not taken so seriously. And there is Mervyn Wall, who ceased to publish anything for a number of years and suffered neglect as a consequence. And James Plunkett, who achieved instant renown with *Strumpet City*. And Bryan MacMahon, a Kerryman like John B. Keane, and with the same true eye and ear for Irish country matters.

And – and – and – The first bookshop one enters in Ireland will have an 'Irish' section bristling with Irish writers deserving of notice, such as John Montague, John Jordan, Bernard Farrell, Brendan Kennelly, Eavan Boland, Thomas Kinsella, John Hewitt, Richard Murphy, Eugene McCabe, Monk Gibbon, Ulick O'Connor, Neil Jordan, John MacGahern; names taken almost at random from a group that could be multiplied three and four times over. Nor of course are they all equal in merit or in present reputation, nor are their present reputaions any true indication of their future status. Some are already old, some are very young, with much yet to achieve. And to attempt to pick the eventual giants out of the fifty or a hundred present contenders for the mantles of Shaw and Yeats and Joyce and Flann O'Brien would be ridiculous for anyone, let alone for me. But let me say at once, before ES can hit me on the head with a bound volume of *Ireland's Own*, that never in the long history of the country has there existed so brilliant a galaxy of polished talent – no, genius. Each name as one considers it outshines the others, only to be unjustly dimmed in its turn as one regards another new Dante from Rathmines, or Tralee, or Belturbet, or Cork city. And the critics! Plutarch hides his head among the shades. Cicero grants himself vanquished by their golden pens, the justice of their opinions, the majesty of their expressions.

(ES: Now you're talking. Go on. Don't be shy. *Praise* them. They won't mind.

C: Could I say anything critical at all? Just a sentence? To – sort of balance things?

ES: No no no no NO! You'll ruin everything. You always do. Just tell the truth and forget about being clever. Who was this man Plutarch, anyway? He sounds as if he wrote pornography. Where did he come from?

C: Greece.

ES: I knew it. You're supposed to be writing about Ireland. *Write* about Ireland.'

C: I'll try. And not a word of criticism shall pass my lips. Let me tell you about an utterly uncontroversial Irish writer. Let me tell me about Laetitia Pilkington, who has for a long time been undeservedly neglected as a writer. She was born in 1712 –

ES: I won't have it! She was a loose woman!

C: She was not so, a loose woman. That was a dirty slander. Her husband found her in bed with a man, one has to admit, but she had a perfect explanation.

ES: I'd like to hear it, the trollop!

C: You shall, you shall. She had borrowed this book from this man and he didn't want to leave it with her overnight and she wanted to finish it and so she read it into the wee hours of the morning and because it was cold she got into bed to go on reading and this man was cold too – the man that owned the book – and so *he* got into bed beside her –

ES: Stop! I won't hear another word!

C: That's what her husband said when he came in and found them. He divorced her because of it, but it was very unjust. All her friends agreed it was. They set her up in a boutique in Chelsea after she left Dublin –

ES: I'll bet they did, the strap.

C: And she went bankrupt and there was a subscription among her admirers and she wrote her memoirs and – it's a very interesting story.

ES: It's a *disgusting* story. Don't you know any pure stories?

C: I'm sorry I started this book at all.

ES: Not half as sorry as I am.)

Where was I? Laetitia Pilkington. All right. Let's forget about her. The trouble is that no one – not even someone who is qualified, which I am not – can sensibly discuss a whole literature in one book, let alone in one chapter of one book. And there is a lot of Irish literature to discuss, from 'St Patrick's Breast-Plate', the famous 5th-century hymn, onwards. Irish literature, with Greek, has the longest continuous history in Europe, and even Anglo-Irish literature goes back to the 15th century. And there is a pleasant theory that Irish literature and Irish poets had a deep and decisive influence on Icelandic literature.

It is certainly odd that the Icelandic sagas and poetry are so dramatically different from their supposed parent, Old Norse poetry. Between the stiff court poetry of medieval Norway and the fresh lyricism of Icelandic poetry there are two worlds of difference. The theory is that that difference was caused by Icelandic exposure to Irish literature, through trade with Dublin, and the bringing of Irish poetry and a startlingly new way of approaching story-telling, new at least as far as the Icelanders were concerned. Hence the great and sudden, and otherwise unexplained, flourishing of the sagas and a new kind of Icelandic poetry.

Did Snorre Sturlason, for example, hear old Irish slaves recite Irish sagas by winter firesides, sagas translated into Norse? There need have been no difficulty about the translations, since old Norse or Norron was a *lingua franca* understood and spoken across Northern Europe, from Limerick to Lindisfarne to Novgorod. An illustration of this is provided by the story of Harold Gillekrist (the name means 'Servant of Christ'), the Irish boy who became the ancestor of all the subsequent Norwegian kings, and a good many of the Danish and Swedish ones as well. (Incidentally, is it not extraordinary that the most democratic countries in the world are the ones to have kept monarchies?) Harold Gillekrist's mother was an Irishwoman, raped on a 12th-century night near Belfast by the Norse king and Viking raider Magnus Bareleg. How unwilling she was to be raped is not known, but one hopes that it was by agreement. But Magnus sailed away, as unmarried fathers often do, to be justifiably killed very soon afterwards, and the lady gave birth to Harold after due delay. Nineteen years later she told him that it was time to seek his fortune and claim his birthright. Accordingly he went down to the shore, where some Norse merchants were trading, and bargained for a passage to Norway. Evidently he had no trouble in making himself understood, nor did he on arrival in Norway, where eventually, after many exciting adventures he became king.

One last detail about Harold, before I abandon him, throws light, if not on language or literature, at least on Irish life and drinking habits.

(ES: I'm warning you!

C: No, no, wait! This story is on *our* side.

ES: It had better be!)

Well. As may be imagined, Harold's arrival, announcing his royal status, was not particularly welcome to his half-brother, Sigurd, by then king in succession to Magnus. And the welcome was even more diminished by young Harold continually boasting about how much better at everything the Irish were when compared to the Norwegians. He claimed, among other things, that some Irishmen could outrun the fastest Norwegian horsesmen.

At this his half-brother said he could make good his boast or have his throat cut, whichever he liked. Useless for Harold to protest that he hadn't said *he* could do it, only that *some* Irishmen could do it. He was dragged to the starting-point, and matched against one of the king's sons, mounted on the finest of horses. the race was to be run along a course that is now the main street of Oslo, running up to the Cathedral, or so I believe. And despite some despicable trickery on the part of his enemies, he won his bet. He also won some equally unequal contests at swimming. And the point of all this is the explanation, given in the Norse chronicles, that the Norwegians were in a lamentable physical condition because they ate and drank far too much, while the abstemious Irish could outrun and outswim them because they were naturally in the pink of condition.

(ES: All this is a lie, isn't it? You're making it up?

C: Scout's honour. It's all there in black and white in the *Heims Kringla*.

ES: I don't trust you – when you're yourself I know where I am. But when you get all mealy-mouthed ... Why don't you write about Connemara?

C: You mean about all the new bungalows and neo-Georgian villas dotting the bogs? The ones with the Ionic porticoes? And the caravan sites?

ES: I'm warning you for the last time –)

Literature. Yes. Well. One problem about modern Irish literature is to know where it should be going, what it should be doing. Celebrating Ireland?

(ES: Yes! Yes!

C: But isn't that a narrow and confining aim?

ES: No! No!

C: Should it not seek rather to be universal, rooted in Ireland perhaps, but spreading its interest as far afield as humanity itself?

ES: I don't like the sound of this at all. Why don't you tell them about Donegal? No – no. Don't. But that's enough about literature. I never did trust books. Tell them about the economy.

C: You mean the fact that per head our foreign borrowing is now the biggest in Europe? That we owe above £3,000 for every man, woman and child in the country? That we haven't a hope in Heaven of paying it all off and that –

ES: If I had a gun I'd shoot you. Tell them about the Industrial Development Authority. All the foreign industries that come flocking here because of our scenery and our lovely skies and clear streams, and our skilled and willing workers and our tax advantages and our economic subsidies and –

C: And the 30 per cent failure rate? And the bankruptcies? And the way some of the foreigners float off as soon as they've milked the last subsidy out of the government?

ES: This chapter is supposed to be about literature.

C: It was you who told me to stop talking about books. Shall I tell them about how the farmers thought the EEC was going to be the Coming of the Kingdom and how in the last three or four years farm incomes are down 50 per cent. Yerra.

ES: Tell them about Dublin. Dublin's Fair City. The parks. The broad streets which were the first examples of Town Planning in Europe. The stately Georgian terraces, each with a subtly varied roof line so that no one house is identical with its neighbours ...

C: You mean those old houses in Fitzwilliam Street that the Electricity Supply Board pulled down years ago? Or the ones that that other crowd pulled down in St Stephen's Green?

ES: At least you could tell them about the fine new buildings. Adventurous, exciting designs blending the best of the future with the wonderful traditions of our Celtic past –

C: You mean like the American Embassy, the one like a Celtic biscuit tin with a moat round it?

ES: Have you no single decent thing to say about any aspect of Irish life? Except the Guinness, I suppose. You writers are all the same. Drunken degenerates.

C: You get better Guinness in Belgium than you do in Ireland. Export stuff. The only real pint of Guinness I ever had in my life was in Belgium.

ES: You've run out of space. This is the end of the chapter about literature. Goodnight.)

8 A Question of Culture

The Irish countryside is generally accepted as being among the few uncontestable advantages of living in Ireland, and a prime reason for coming here for a holiday. Unfortunately we in Ireland accept these truths only on a purely intellectual level, as expressed in Tourist Board advertisements and conversational clichés. At a gut level, where we might actually be in a position to do something about preserving the beauty, it is a different story.

Some of us do indeed recognise that our surroundings now belong to us and no longer to the hated foreigner, and therefore that those surroundings ought to be kept clean and decent. Almost everyone, however, feels that the cleanliness and decency is someone else's responsibility, not ours. We demand that the government do something, or the local council. But no one wants to help, even at the lowest level of not littering the streets, or by helping to pick up the litter that other freedom-loving Irish citizens scatter broadcast. Men on the dole would be horrified at the idea of being asked to take a shovel and spend a day or two clearing up some local eyesore, or clearing away the years's one heavy snowfall. No one wants someone else to build an ugly office block in their neighbourhood, but everyone claims the right to build an ugly bungalow in the middle of a beauty spot. Or to decorate it with bursting plastic sacks of rubbish or an abandoned motor car or a corrugated iron shed.

Irish towns and villages look so frightful that there is a national campaign – a highly unsuccessful one, to all appearances – called the 'Tidy Towns' competition. Even the name of it indicated a feeble pessimism in the face of rubbish-strewn ugliness, as if the height of Irish ambition at the municipal level was not beauty, or even cleanliness, but a momentary tidiness, an annual hair-combing and doing-up of buttons. To be followed two days later by a renewed orgy of scattered iced lolly papers, empty cigarette packets, old newspapers, dog dirt, broken bottles, take-away food cartons, torn mattresses, vandalised telephone kiosks, broken public benches, and piles of uncollected refuse.

'Litter is a crying shame. Stop it', whimpers a tepidly hopeful advertisement. The problem is not 'litter', it is sheer filth, and public squalor. And public indifference to squalor. Even the protesters, even those who want something done about it – by someone else – are in a tiny minority. The average Irish man – and woman – and child – regard the outside world as a convenient extension of the kitchen dustbin.

(ES: It's a lie, a dirty lie. Wash your mouth out with soap. If you're not careful, I'll see you're forced to attend Feiseanna* every weekend for the next three months. As if the beauty of Ireland's unspoilt scenery is not world renowned. From the cliffs of Moher to –

C: I only mean –

ES: You mean trouble. That's what you mean, Cleeve.

C: I just want –

ES: I've some friends who know how to deal with the likes of you. They do a special line in concrete boots, so if there's any more of this rubbish ...

C: There won't be, I promise. I'll read *Ireland's Own* every night. I'll go out and kiss a tourist. If I can find one. I'll –

ES: Well might you. Take yourself to Bunratty. Learn to play the harp and the penny whistle and the one-stringed fiddle. Learn to serve foaming tankards of medieval mead at medieval tourist banquets in the medieval tourist banqueting hall. Go and apologise to a medieval tourist. It's the likes of you have this country in the state it's in.)

Bunratty? Ah, Bunratty!

* Festivals of traditional Irish music, song and dance.

Bunratty, for the sake of the stone ignorant, is a fine Norman castle situate some five miles from the estuary, near the city of Limerick. It has all mod cons, h&c, OFCH, table d'hôte, à la carte, plus a delightful staff of waiters and waitresses and entertainers all dressed in Dublin's idea of Hollywood's idea of Irish medieval costume. There, for a handful of American Express cards (sure and begorrah, asthore, that will do nicely) you can wine and sup and dine and be entertained, and get your ear bent crooked by medieval Irish music and your belly filled with medieval Irish sucking-pig. Medieval jesters will make medieval Irish jokes for you. Medieval Irish prisoners will be medievally tortured for you. If you have a Diner's Card as well as an American Express Card, and belong to Rotary, you may even be chosen as Lord of the Banquet for the evening and wear an Irish medieval coronet.

I'm not absolutely sure why, but I find this whole gallimaufry intensely distasteful, not to say appallingly vulgar, and I'm sorry that we've felt it necessary to descend to it. I find it even more tasteless than Morris dances arranged for tourists in Devonshire, and that's saying a lot. When a nation begins to sell its past, particularly a falsified, tarted-up travesty of its past, then I begin to wonder about its future. Am I just a sour old man, with no sense of humour, or of innocent fun? (ES: Yes! Yes! You didn't even want to go to the Rolling Stones concert! You're morally dead. Go and get buried.)

Perhaps that's good advice. For whenever I compare the modern vulgarities of Irish life – anglicised, americanised, hamburgerised – with the little I know of the realities of the past, I feel cheapened and ashamed. It's no one's fault. And everyone's fault, mine included. Everyone wants junk food, and junk TV, and disposable cans of soft drinks, and plastic bags – let us be honest and stop talking about Irish culture. Compare Bunratty to any scrap of our real past, Ireland's real past.

Yeats wrote long ago: 'We too had good attendance once, Hearers and hearteners of the work, Aye, horsemen for companions. Before the merchant and the clerk breathed on the world with timid breath.' Today those very merchants and clerks seem like princes of high culture compared to our present generation. A year or so ago Dublin Corporation and the Irish Government distinguished themselves by destroying the finest unexcavated Viking settlement site in Western

Europe, perhaps anywhere, in order to allow an office block to be built, which could have been built anywhere else. Due to various follies and oversights there might – there *might* – have been heavy compensation to be paid, a million pounds or so. But Knock airport? To look no further into the wastelands of government squandermania. (Present costs of this white elephant are around £9 million, due to increase to a figure variously calculated as from £18 million to £35 million, with a large annual subsidy on top. The rationale is that the pilgrimage centre at Knock requires an airport to service the crowds of pilgrims arriving there. Few impartial observers agree.) But there were votes in Knock airport – a few, anyway. There were none in archaeology. Only our past, now destroyed for ever.

I bring you news,
The stag is lowing,
Winter descends
Summer is gone

The cold has gripped
The birds' wings,
Season of ice,
That is my news. *

It is my news too. If you want to find 'Irish culture' do not come to Ireland. Read old books. Read about the ancient Gaelic world. Read about the Wild Geese who chose exile in the 17th century. Gaelic chiefs with their servants and followers who went to France and Spain and Rome and Austria to serve in any army rather than the English, while at home their castles were occupied by carpetbaggers with new names and no manners, and their woods were cut down so that even poor vagabonds might find no shelter. Read about the poets who had served the chieftains, and who now descended among the people to scratch a living as hedge schoolmasters. If you have any feelings for the past, spend them on such stories, and not in Bunratty. Spend them on the story of the great 18th-century poet Eoghan rua Ó Suilleabháin of the Silver Tongue, who earned his living as a spailpín (a day labourer) at 6d and 7d a day.

* From a 9th-century poem, translated by the late Professor David Greene.

Unlike an earlier generation of exiles who went into service in continental armies or navies, he joined the English navy and was at the battle off Dominica where Admiral Rodney defeated the French. In celebration of the victory he wrote a long panegyric called *Rodney's Glory*, in doggerel English, a language he knew very poorly and for which he had no feeling. Admiral Rodney, to whom he presented the poem and who rewarded him with a purse, must have smiled in cultured scorn at the presumptuousness of this poor Irish barbarian imagining he could write poetry. But in Irish Eoghan Rua is reckoned the equal of Keats or Shelley. Or perhaps a more accurate comparison is with Robert Burns.

But he was one of the last of the true succession of Irish poets. Only Blind Raftery was still to come, and that strange, ambiguous figure, the author of *The Midnight Court*, Brian Merriman, schoolmaster and satirist, mathematician and Irish Rabelais. For nearly two hundred years his tremendous poem has horrified the pious and delighted poetry lovers. In the 1930s any attempt to translate it wholly and honestly into English was resisted by the Censorship Board with bell, book and candle.

> Everyone's heart some priest extolled
> For the lonesome women that he consoled;
>
> Any day now it may be revealed
> That the Cardinals have it signed and sealed,
> And we'll hear no more of the ban on marriage
> Before the priests go entirely savage.

And this was written in the 1780s!

Read these things if you want an idea of the real Irish culture. Read *The Islandman* by Tomás Ó Crohán (translated by Robin Flower and reprinted by the Oxford University Press at least as late as 1978).

Read Peig Sayers' life story, *Peig* (translated by Bryan MacMahon). Read *Twenty Years A-Growing* by Maurice O'Sullivan (translated by M. Llewelyn Davies and G. Thomson) – read a hundred books, a few of which are listed in Appendix D. Read Frank O'Connor's anthology of Irish poetry, *Kings Lords and Commons*, all in his own translation. Read Daniel Corkery's *The Hidden*

Ireland, read – but look in the Appendix.

Of course, talking of books, there is another kind of Irish culture (really a Dublin culture) that certain sorts of visitors long to find. This is the pub culture which, like *Punch*, never has been what it was. Middle-aged Danes and balding Americans return to Dublin twenty years after their days as students in Trinity College – or come for the first time armed with a copy of *Ulysses* and an enormous thirst – moist-eyed and gabbling about the Dublin pubs, and the wonderful talk to be heard in them and the wonderful characters to be found in them and worshipfully observed.

'Is Neary's still what it was? And McDaid's? And Davy Byrne's? And the Pearl Bar? And ... and ... and ... ' Asking the native Dubliner about places he's never heard of and people he's never met, and would never want to meet, drunk or sober.

'You mean to tell me Flann O'Brien is dead? Myles? The one and only Myles? And Paddy Kavanagh? Of course Behan – even at home we know Behan is dead. Is *everybody* dead?'

Yes and no. I was never a pub goer, and so I have to take on trust the endless stories of the great crack there was in them in the old days. But once or twice, when I worked in Irish television, one or another of these legendary characters would lurch into a studio to be interviewed, and any mental experience more painful than trying to interview a sadly drunken poet on television must be very painful indeed.

I once was condemned to interview a small boy and his dog for four minutes. The four minutes were fixed and irrevocable. Nothing could be done to shorten them. Nothing was available to replace the boy or the dog. Why should there be? The dog did wonderful tricks. The small boy had sworn it on the telephone. And my editor was a credulous man. Of course, faced with TV lights, three cameras and eight strangers the dog forgot every trick he ever knew, if he ever did know any, which I doubt, and on TV the small boy was as near a deaf mute as makes no difference, in spite of his fluency on the telephone. It was a long four minutes. But nothing like so long as any single minute of attempting to interview a belching, dribbling, maundering ruin who had once been a great writer.

(Of course, modern poets are not at all like that. Truly. I mean it. Don't tell ES I said *anything* about poets. Old or new, she doesn't like them being mentioned.)

But this pub talk. Every time I go into a pub, which isn't often – to buy a box of matches or to use the gents – I don't see anyone talking at all. A row of sombre men at the bar looking as if they've lost money at the races. Three young executives having a sandwich lunch and reading the financial pages of the *Irish Times*. A courting couple sharing a Gaelic Coffee. Not a poet in sight. No crack. No epigrams. No repartee. I probably choose the wrong pubs, of course, not having crack as my first priority.

And no doubt there has been, and maybe there still is, brilliant pub talk here or there. It's a famous fact of Irish literary life that many Irish writers have been better at talking about their books than at actually writing them. Many's the masterpiece that has been scrawled illegibly by drunken fingers dipped in Guinness on the pub counter, only to be wiped away come closing time by the bar curate.

However, this is a side of Irish life to which I am tone deaf, and if you wish to hear it praised you must go to someone else.

(ES: You are tone deaf to every side of Irish life. Go home to London.

C: I am not so. I like the scenery.

ES: You do not! You were complaining only yesterday about the corrugated iron roofs and the abandoned motor cars. And the bungalows. And going on about the pig slurry killing the trout in the rivers. Aren't pigs more important than trout? Isn't there more nourishment in them?

C: There is indeed, ma'am. Indeed there is. Buckets more. But couldn't we put the pig slurry somewhere else besides in with the trout?

ES: Where else, you gombeen? And have the farmers complaining about that too? Haven't they enough on their minds, the poor divils, without being tormented about where they tip their pig slurry?

C: And their silage.

ES: There you go again. Always the hard word. Always the unkind crack. Where were you brought up?

C: In London.

ES: I knew it. A sassenach. A sassenach camouflaging his mean little soul with a bunch of shamrock, pretending to be Irish. You make me sick. What else do you like about Ireland?

C: I like the people.

ES: God between us and all harm! The people? You like the *people*? Tell me when you ever said a good word about any living Irish soul unless they were a hundred years dead? You don't even like James Joyce.

C: I don't understand him.

ES: No decent person does. I'm not talking about *reading* him. I'm talking about *admiring* him. He is a World Figure. Ireland is proud of him. We're getting a firm in Hong Kong to make little wee dolls of him in genuine simulated bog oak, smoking a pipe and decorated with shamrocks.

C: I don't think he smoked a pipe.

ES: There you go again! Always destructive! Sarcastic! I bet your mother was ashamed of you.

C: I'm sorry. I think James Joyce was the ruin of modern Irish writing. Every eejit from then to now has been trying to copy him. Do you remember the millionaire who used to issue his company's annual reports in the style of Joyce? His fellow directors had kittens every year.

ES: I will not listen to this stuff. You're a disgrace to hack writers.)

Indeed I do like the scenery, and I do like the people. Despite what the people are doing to the scenery. It's fair to say that the only thing that has saved the scenery is that there is a lot of it compared to the number of people, and until recently the people have lacked the means and the energy to destroy it. The beauty of the Irish countryside is very largely the beauty of neglect. Ruined cottages. Hedges run wild. Hillsides abandoned to gorse and heather. But let the local inhabitants get their hands on money and machines and the vandalism begins. The hedges are chopped as if they were man's mortal enemies. New bungalows and villas of startlingly hideous and totally inappropriate design stud the fields like ugly mushrooms. Heather and gorse are replaced by mud and rubbish. Noble trees are savagely uprooted. Supermarkets like cement aircraft hangars are built to provide plastic bags and bottles with which to decorate the roads.

Thirty years ago a famous Swedish report commissioned by the then Irish government said, in effect, that we were visually illiterate.

The main result of this report – at least the one most visible to the public – is the Kilkenny Design Centre, imaginatively housed in the one-time stables of Kilkenny Castle. Artists and designers will have their own opinions about the Design Centre's work and influence, but to the layman's eye their work bears the solid, not to say stolid, imprint of their Scandinavian begetters. Plain silver and blonde wood, so to speak, excellent in itself, but Hiberno-Norse rather than native Hibernian. Although any aesthetically minded English reader, sitting in his William Morris print chair while his wife dries the dishes with a Tower of London souvenir tea-cloth, can hardly afford to sneer. I doubt if any country has ever successfully revived its past artistic heritage once it has died.

No one today would be so flattering as to describe us as visually illiterate. Fine Georgian buildings rouse developers, and architects, and councillors, and the responsible government ministers to a competitive fury of hatred and destruction.

There is indeed a type of mind in Ireland that does truly see a Georgian building or an avenue of 18th-century beech trees and elms as something which it is virtuous to destroy. 'The Ascendancy built them, planted them, enjoyed them. We'll destroy them, to show our hatred of the Ascendancy, of the old masters, of the 700 years of English rule and misrule.' It is useless arguing with such people. One can only pray that they do not get their way too often.

But very often they did, and do, either by bomb and arson, or via the local council's planning department, so that Ireland's stock of desirable houses is diminished still further. (As I write this Drogheda Corporation is preparing to demolish one of the last three 17th-century town houses to survive in Ireland, to accommodate a road scheme that could easily be altered to spare the house. One reason for this act of vandalism is that the house is not even listed as a building worthy of preservation. Not because it is not worthy, but because no one was sufficiently interested to see that it was listed. No doubt it is sheer oversight on someone's part that the other two houses have survived. It might be dangerous to say where they are in case they are immediately knocked down to make way for hamburger outlets.)

Even our coinage hasn't survived. Once regarded, and rightly so, as unique in the world for its imaginative beauty, it has since been bastardised and destroyed by the Department of Finance, or whatever bunch of cretins it is that decides such matters. The background to this recent vandalism makes a longish story, but one worth telling.

In 1926 the Irish government took a most extraordinary and indeed unique decision – no less than to design an entire coinage for the new state. Until then, of course, in spite of the Troubles and the Civil War and the setting up of the Free State, English coins had circulated in Ireland as legal tender – and, naturally, as the only tender, there being no other. The Free State Government then decided, in spite of a thousand apparently more pressing needs and problems, to commission someone to provide us with a new coinage.

It is difficult to think of a comparable situation. In the recent past other states have often designed single coins to celebrate a great event or a great man, but never a whole coinage. Those single new coins have been obliged to take their place with other existing coins and familiar designs, which must influence and restrict an artist's work. But here was a a whole new coinage, of seven values, from farthing to half-crown, to celebrate and illustrate the interests and nature of the new state. It was a prospect to excite any artist.

Until the artist reflected that the decisions would rest with a committee set up by a government, and a government moreover that consisted not of public-school and university men who knew their Virgil (as governments should), but of ex-gunmen. One of the most wonderful artistic opportunities of modern times had fallen into the blood-stained hands of a gang of ex-assassins.

(ES: Hold on there! Hold on! Maybe they were the Other Crowd. And blood-stained hands is right enough. Look at the seventy men they shot – every one of them a real Republican and belonging to the Real Crowd. And Erskine Childers, murdered as sure as murder is murder. But they're *our* assassins, and you don't want to go and be saying things like that to a bunch of foreigners who don't understand the first thing about Ireland. Cross that out.

C: All right. I'll start again –

ES: Not from the beginning! Just from 'fallen into the hands of' – you could say 'a crowd of narrow backs', if you like. Or West Brits. Or slieveens. Or seaneens. Or jackeens. I don't mind that. Only not assassins. In the Establishment you have to learn to avoid the truth.

The first thing I learned when I joined the Civil Service –

C: You didn't join in the great days, you being as young as you are. Do you know that in the times we're speaking of – that'd be 1926 and around then, the men used to keep chamber pots in their offices, behind screens, and on a Friday night, when they'd have been preparing for the weekend with a jar or two, you'd see the steam rising over the tops of the screens like the mists over Ben Bulben and Slieve na Mon. And the smell of ammonia and Guinness would petrify a cat. It's why they didn't want women to join the service. It would have created untold difficulties.

ES: Liar! Blasphemer! Judas! You're being paid to say these things! You're employed by the CIA to ruin Ireland's sacred neutrality, and undermine the nation's right to –

C: I'm not! I'm not! An old civil servant told me that, on my word of honour.

ES: I'll report you to the Court of Human Rights. I'll –

C: Cross my heart and hope to die. It was the same man told me about them keeping revolvers in their in-trays. He said if you went into an office when they weren't expecting you you'd find yourself staring down the barrels of two or three Webley .45s and hear the hammers clicking back. He was a tea boy then and he said it gave him the jitters every afternoon.

ES: For pity's sake get on with the coinage. You were at 'fallen into the hands of –'

C: Right – had fallen into the hands of a group of men not at all likely to be stirred by artistic considerations, and indeed, from their background in revolutionary politics, more likely to be Philistines.

ES: I like that. Yes. It sounds educated. Have you spelt it right?

C: I think so.

ES: Shouldn't there be an F there in Filistines?

C: Not according to the dictionary. Can I go on?

ES: Yes. But stay careful. No cracks.

C: What must have been that artistic observer's amazement and delight when he saw the government of the Free State hand the task of selecting the designs and of choosing the artists to no less a figure than the great Irish poet and, at that time, Free State senator, William Butler Yeats.

ES: Is this true?

C: I swear it. It is one of the most extraordinary and wonderful incidents in modern Irish governmental history.

ES: I don't like it. A poet? The Real Crowd would never have done a thing like that. What sort of poetry did this man write?

C: Good poetry. 'A terrible beauty is born'. That sort of thing.

ES: I still don't like it. But you'd better get on.

C: An equally extraordinary thing is that, within nine months from being set up, the Committee under the chairmanship of Senator Yeats had decided upon the designs they wanted, had chosen seven world-renowned artists to offer examples of the way each would like to execute the designs, had received the examples and chosen the ones they considered most suitable. A year later, in 1928, the coins were in the hands of the public, and a more beautiful *set* of coins – as opposed to individual specimens – can scarcely have been seen since the days of ancient Sicily and Athens.

ES: Bravo! And this set of coins – where is it now? Why don't we know about it?

C: You do know about it. It is in your purse. At least, the remains of it. When they started this decimal coinage business they ruined the set.

ES: You're pulling my leg. You mean our coins with the fish and the cow on them? And the copper ones with squiggles?

C: The squiggles are from *The Book of Kells*, and they are a lunatic addition to our coinage imposed on it by the Real Crowd, who have as much artistic sense as a shoal of haddock. I'm talking about our real coinage, of which the salmon and the bull are the last wonderful remains. We had the Irish hunter on the half-crown, the Irish salmon on the florin, the Irish bull on the shilling, the Irish wolfhound on the sixpence, the Irish hare on the threepenny bit, the Irish hen on the penny, the Irish sow on the halfpenny, and, perhaps most beautiful of all, the Irish woodcock on the farthing. Sic transit gloria Hiberniae. Now we have squiggles. But it *was* glorious.

ES: I wish I had never allowed you to start any of this. Hiberniae. You're making a jeer again. And in French too, just to show off.

C: I'm not making a jeer. The best of this story is yet to come, though. Wait till I tell you. This wonderful achievement of artistic creativity and this almost unique example of governmental imagination might have been expected to delight the Plain People.

And even the critics. Alas, not so. Criticism abounded, of the most venomous kind, and I here append a brief account of it written by one of the Committee members and chief victims of the attacks, Dr Thomas Bodkin, at that time one of the Governors of the National Gallery of Ireland, and subsequently its Director:

Though we all realised that the new coinage could not, despite its excellence, escape the criticism which every public venture in Ireland inevitably produces, none of us expected that such criticism would be mainly directed to our failure to identify God and Mammon.

Two years ago, at the commencement of our sittings, we had invited the public to suggest emblems or symbols suitable for reproduction on the coins. We did not receive suggestions of religious emblems from anyone, with the exception of a lady, who advised the portrayal of 'a kneeling angel pouring money from a sack'! ...

It was only on the eve of the issue of the coinage that the first rumblings of abuse were heard ...

The Cathedral Chapter of Tuam, with Monsignor Macken in the chair, found time to pass a resolution declaring:

'That we consider the designs of the proposed new coins utterly unsuited for the coinage of this ancient Christian nation ... '

A gentleman signing himself 'Beppo', and described by the Editor of the *Irish Independent* as an Irish priest, wrote:

'If these pagan symbols once get a hold, then is the thin edge of the wedge of Freemasonry sunk into the very life of our Catholicity, for the sole object of having these pagan symbols instead of religious emblems on our coins is to wipe out all trace of religion from our minds, to forget the "Land of the Saints", and beget a land of devil-worshippers, where evil may reign supreme.'

Another critic detected in our proceedings 'a turning down of God'.

Numerous writers, in a strange confusion of ideas, seemed to argue that the divine work of creation was, on the fifth and part of the sixth day, handed over to the Devil. They forgot to ask themselves what St Francis would have thought of such heresy, or St Thomas, who speaks of animals as 'the footprints of God, by which we learn of His existence'. Surely it is only a pagan who would associate our shilling (carrying the bull) with Mithras or with Apis rather than with St Matthew. To such critics we feel inclined to say: Did God who made the hen make thee?

In an earlier lecture Dr Bodkin had, as he says, set out the Committee's reasons for avoiding either nationalistic or religious designs on the coins, and had also pointed out the lack of advice it had received from the public.

> Individual members of the public showed little or no inclination to assist us. We put a notice in the papers inviting their co-operation. Our invitation was practically ignored. This notice was later supplemented by an advertisement in which we complained mildly of public apathy. That apathy continued. So, let any individual who may be prepared to criticise adversely our selection of designs consider whether he is justified in doing so by virtue of having offered us valuable advice which we rejected.

> One good result, at least, has flowed from this controversy – the general admission that the coinage is artistically excellent. This admission is tacit in Ireland. Other countries have not hesitated to give it vocal expression. Thus, the critic of the *Manchester Guardian* wrote: 'I think that the Irish coinage will be acknowledged as the most beautiful in the modern world ... I doubt if any country but Ireland would have had the imagination and freedom to lay down the conditions that would have made such designs possible.' The critic of the *Nation* declared: 'The Free State has the most beautiful set of coins in the world.' The critic of the *Evening Standard* admitted: 'We may well be jealous of the beautiful new Irish coins.'

> The Committee appreciate such generous praise, though it would have been still more welcome had it come from their own

countrymen, particularly as we have plenty of reason to believe that the opinions of our English critics are shared by the vast majority of intelligent Irish men and women.

Is it necessary to add much comment? Here in a nutshell – well, a rather large nutshell, say a coconut shell – there is an illustration of the paradoxical nature of Irish life: culture attacked by ignorance, cultivated and selfless minds beset by yahoos, idealism crassly misunderstood and trampled underfoot by –

ES: Will you stop? You told that whole boring load of rubbish for the one sole purpose of getting at us again. The Plain Decent People of Ireland regard money as money, not as pansified, Frenchified, dolled-up little bits of works of art. I hate art. Every decent Irish woman and man hates art. It's foreign. It's English. It's immoral. Nakedness. Indecency. There are pictures there in that National Gallery that I wouldn't want any respectable human being to be obliged to look at. And right next door to Dáil Eireann, where our beloved leader is trying to keep the country on an even keel and face the storms of the future and plough a straight furrow and leave no stone unturned for the prosperity of the agricultural community and the advancement of industry and commerce and to waken the nation to the dawning of a new day and doing away with the doom and gloom of the Other Crowd to bring back the bloom and boom of the Real Party – and you here drivelling about art and poets and professors and woodcock. As to which any fool can see it's a snipe.

C: It's not a snipe. It's a woodcock.

ES: I don't care if it's a parrot. A good dose of number 7 shot is what'd settle its feathers for it. Art! I've warned you once, and I'll warn you twice, and I won't warn you three times. Find something plain and straight and decent to say about this country that gives you bread and shelter, or else.

C: Well, what about our great theatrical tradition? D'you remember the Tennessee Williams play they put on at the Pike, where they arrested the actress on the stage for having a contraceptive? A guard had to sit and watch the play on purpose so he could catch her at it. That was a great moment in theatrical history, like the riots in the Abbey over the *Playboy*, do you remember *them*? When Yeats shouted at the audience 'You've disgraced yourselves again!' — or was that at the riot over *The Shadow of a Gunman* when the audience objected to the National Flag being taken into a pub? Oh, great moments! Great moments! The English never riot at plays, they haven't the soul for it.

ES: Will you stop! The *Playboy* riots! When were you last in a theatre?

C: Fifteen — no I'm a liar, sixteen years ago — no, I'm a liar again, it must be nearer twenty. When the old earl was still alive, the fat one, the *real* Lord Longford. Not the new one that looks after the prisons. The old one that looked after the theatres. Did you know he used to eat the menu round twice when he went out to dinner? He said he needed it. The girl'd bring him his coffee and ask what he'd take with it, and he'd say 'The soup again' and he'd go right through the whole lot all over, the second time. He was a *man*. And he used to stand on the steps where you went into the stalls, with a little collecting box for the 'Save the Gate Theatre' fund. It was difficult to get past him without putting something in the box, him being so fat. And an earl too. But they were great plays he put on. Molière. Beaumarchais. Plays with a beginning and a middle and an end. You knew where you were with them. Not like these modern things with girls running about in their knickers and fellows singing songs and ringing bells and making things up as they go along. And Anew MacMaster. Do you remember *him*? A real prince of the theatre. *Othello*! He used to black himself all over, even under his tights. He said the farmers expected it. Playing *Hamlet* in villages that hadn't seen Charlie Chaplin, let alone Shakespeare. *King Lear*! The girls playing Goneril and Regan — it'd be as much as their lives were worth to let themselves be seen after the show. They'd by lynched for treating their father like that. Oh, the old days, the old days! The Fit-ups! *Macbeth* with three actors and two actresses, and the whole thing cut to fifty minutes. *Maria Marten in the Red Barn*. Sweeney Todd. *The Colleen Bawn*. Oh, the theatre is in ruins this past twenty years. TV has killed it stone dead.

ES: Are you finished?

C: And Michael MacLiammoir. And Hilton Edwards. And Orson Welles. And Harold Pinter. And the Gaiety girls. And the Royalettes.

Kicking up their legs till you'd think they'd drop. There's nothing like it these days. Just bingo halls. Roller discos. It's the end of civilisation.

ES: It's not. It's the end of this chapter.)

9 Crime

Thirty years ago crime in Ireland was mostly a village constable affair. Stolen bicycles were about the height of it. No one bothered to lock a front door at night. The guards in country places could occupy their time hunting for illicit poteen, with now and then the triumph of finding a still. Ireland was a peaceful village, and if some scallywag was caught having stolen his fifth bicycle and brought to judgement, the district justice as likely as not would offer him the choice of going to gaol or going to England.

(ES: That is a flat, libellous, slanderous, wicked lie, worse than all the others rolled into one. It is a well known fact that our system of justice is the best and fairest and most impartial and even-handed and honest in the civilised world. From the days of the Druids, and St Columba, and the Brehon Laws, Irish judges, Irish Law, Irish criminals, have been noted for their Celtic purity –

C: I was only making a joke. But it *did* happen. Often. The English used to get very vexed about it.

ES: How dare they get vexed? Isn't Irish crime the result of English influence? The Sunday papers –

C: Please!

ES: I'm going to be watching this chapter like a hawk. One more word out of place –

C: I'm trying to tell how pure-hearted Irish criminals and judges were. At one time I can remember, and not so long ago, there were only six women in gaol in the whole of the twenty-six counties. Justices and judges hated sending a woman to gaol, pretty well no matter what she had done.

ES: No Irish woman ever did anything to deserve going to gaol. Unless it was from reading the English papers. And listening to the BBC.)

Maybe not. But one solution to the problem of dealing with women in need of correction – or who, in the eyes of the local justice, needed correction – was to leave the matter in the hands of a convent. By mysterious processes never well defined, women guilty of such peccadilloes as unmarried motherhood combined with poverty – and the two crimes usually went hand in hand (unmarried mothers not guilty of poverty tending to disappear to England) – poor, unmarried mothers often found themselves confined in a convent for quite lengthy periods. First, because the convent was the only available shelter and they themselves sought refuge there. And, later, because there was nowhere else to go, and the convent required them to work off a debt for board and lodging and medical care, usually in the convent laundry, run on a commercial basis for the neighbourhood. Meanwhile the convent would arrange for the baby to be adopted. Not legally adopted, because before the mid sixties no legal adoption existed. But babies were born in convents, and they certainly never grew up in them, or not usually. Rumour had it that a great many of them ended in America.

(ES: That is the filthiest lie of all! The holy nuns! The living images of Christian Charity! And you accusing them of baby farming!

C: I'm not accusing them of anything, except tidying up the mess society left in their laps. Although one could accuse *some* of them – The general Church attitude to illegitimate pregnancy was a long way from compassionate. Girls eight and a half months pregnant made to lie on their bellies on the chapel floor for hours, asking the Blessed Virgin to forgive them. Poor women with their heads shaved. Spending two and three years scrubbing their finger nails off to pay for their keep –

ES: And why wouldn't they pay for their keep, the trollops? As for their heads shaved, did you never hear of head lice, you with your fancy background and your fancy accent? I suppose where you went to school there were no nits?

C: I'm only trying –

ES: Is it not possible for you to say one living word about this country without blackguarding the place? You start a chapter about crime and any Christian writer would begin with bank robberies – carried out by English criminals paid by the English Secret Service to disrupt our economy, incidentally – look at those two brothers who were here, telling the whole world they were sent over by MI27 and the likes of you refusing to believe it –

C: I did so believe it!

ES: Any Christian in the world would have begun with the bank robberies. But not you! Oh no! Not Mr Clever! *He* begins with bicycles just to make a living jeer of a decent, innocent, simple-hearted country that has suffered untold oppression throughout seven centuries of English tyranny – and then you get onto the Church again! The holy nuns! That can't fight back because they have too much dignity and humility and decency and charity and purity, and are occupied day and night in prayer and works of corporal mercy and contemplation and meditation, and teaching the young girls to resist temptation. You're a disgrace to manhood. Even the English would be ashamed of you.

C: I was coming to the bank robberies.

ES: I should hope so! It's a well known fact that more banks have been robbed in Ireland these last years by fewer people than anywhere in the world ever. And fewer of the robberies have been solved and less of the money has been recovered and more guards have been occupied failing to recover it than ever happened before in the history of crime. Irish bank robberies are the admiration of the world, so they are, and if you can't find it in your black heart to admire anything else about this lovely country with its glorious empty roads waiting for tourists to enjoy themselves lingering in the sunshine by trout-filled smiling waters and eating farmhouse teas by roaring turf fires, then at least you can try to admire the bank robberies and stop being so smart for once –

C: I do admire them. But it's not a fair contest. The guards don't have the equipment. There was this robbery in Phibsboro' – I think it was Phibsboro' –

ES: Watch it! Not a dirty cutting remark about Phibsboro' will I allow, that is as decent a place as ever nourished a bank. The inhabitants of Phibsboro' –

C: I know, I know! But this bank robbery – maybe it was in Ballyfermot – anyway, the guards *knew* it was coming off. They got a tip from an informer –

ES: The curse of Ireland on him!

C: So two guards on motorbikes were set to watch the place – there weren't any more guards available, maybe the others were looking after that Grand Duchess and the Grand Duke, or the Aga Khan, or the President –

ES: Watch it! Watch it!

C: I was only trying to make a joke –

ES: Wait till the guards get you down to Pearse Street one of these mornings. You won't be making any little jokes about Grand Duchesses then, I promise you.

C: I know, I know. I'm sorry. I won't do it again. But these two guards were outside the bank – the robbery happened and the two guards radioed for help, but no help arrived because all the other guards were busy, with other bank robberies maybe, if it wasn't the Grand Duchess. So the two guards set off on their motorbikes to chase the robbers, and one of the bikes broke down and the other guard chased on and on and past Kilbarrack – or maybe it was in the other direction – anyway on and on, and the bank robbers just leaned out of the car windows and waved to him goodbye. It was a guard told me the story.

ES: I don't believe a word of it.

C: I'll tell you another story that I got from the same source. About this famous kidnapping, with the kidnappers holed up in a house being besieged by the guards and the journalists of the world there and the guards risking their mortal lives day and night trying to talk the kidnappers out of the place without getting anyone killed in the process. And there was a little machine they needed which would have helped them see exactly what the kidnappers were doing in the room in the house they were locked into with their prisoner. Or maybe it was an extra bit for a machine the guards already had. Anyway, it was a useful object. But it cost £200, so when they asked could they have it the Department said 'No'. But that same week one of the government ministers was having his state Mercedes done over and made bullet proof for several thousand pounds.

ES: And why wouldn't he, the poor man? Isn't his life as valuable as yours? And more valuable by a long shot? And no doubt he not wanting the thing done but his colleagues insisting because of the great value they put on him? Can you never see the true, decent explanation of anything?

C: I can see that no government minister in Ireland has got himself shot since 1926, although one or two could have done with it. But a good few guards have.

ES. You're doing all this to make a jeer of our government. And our bank robbers. You're doing it to make your smart London friends laugh at us.

C: I am not! I was going to say that at least our bank robbers do it all by themselves. The London ones have to have the police to help them.

ES: Good for you! There's a crack! There's one in the eye for the toffee noses! All right, go on, say something else about the English. Say how they rammed our fishing boat with their submarine and didn't own up till they got caught. Say about the strikes in England and the baggage porters at Heathrow and British Leyland. And the way Roy Jenkins talks and how come they didn't know the Argentines were going to invade the Falklands and what happened to their football team in the World Cup and –

C: This book is supposed to be about Ireland.

ES: Make comparisons. Show them up. *There*'s where you can be sarcastic. Talking about the Real Crowd and Our Leader and little battle-axes and split skulls! What about Mr Heath and Mrs T.? What about Mr Foot and Tony Benn? What about Roy Jenkins and the handsome one that has his hair over his eyes? And Mrs Williams and the way she dresses? What about Arthur Scargill and that poor Mr Gormless? *They* could teach you about battle-axes.

C: This chapter has to be about crime.

ES: Then *talk* about crime! Talk about the bank robberies! Bicycles! Girls doing the nuns' laundry! Grand Duchesses! You're a disgrace to the name of hack writer!

C: I'm sorry. Well, the other day some bank robbers in the Limerick area locked the local guards *and* some detectives in their own cell in the Garda Station before they went off to rob the bank –

ES: Stop it! Stop it! Bank robbing is a serious thing. Very serious. It's not a joke, it's a career. It's a profession. Stalin started off as a bank robber and never looked back. Today's bank robber may be tomorrow's Taoiseach. Have *some* respect.

C: I will. I do. But what baffles me is what do they do with the money when they've got it? You and I – if we tried to pay off our overdrafts, the income tax crowd would be down on us like a ton of bricks wanting to know where we got the money. Why don't they ask the bank robbers where they get *their* money?

ES: It all goes to the North for the struggle for a United Ireland. The Establishment doesn't approve of this, in fact it's very vexed about it. But the Plain People – well, you can't go against the will of the Plain People even in the Establishment.

C: I know. I know. But *some* of the bank robbers aren't a bit interested in the struggle for a United Ireland. They're just interested in their own personal struggle for existence as bank robbers. What do *they* do with their money?

ES: I'm not going to get drawn into this. You'll be saying some of them are just plain criminals and gangsters next.

C: I was thinking that, I do admit.

ES: Then don't. The IRA have enough to put up with without you joining in. Change the subject.

C: Well, there are these child pick-pockets in St Stephen's Green. I never saw anything so inefficient in my life. They come up to you with a coat over their hands and push against you, and because of the coat you can't see what their hands are doing, the little wretches. But it's so *obvious*. Of course, they're only about seven years old, and I suppose they'll learn in time.

ES: This is disgusting. Innocent little children!

C: I know it's disgusting. That's why I'm telling about it, in the hope that someone –

ES: Traducing our innocent laughing Irish children! Is nothing at all sacred to you? And them just seeing if you had sweets in your pockets for them, the dear ones, I'll be bound! And you with your dirty sewer of a mind –

C: I still think someone might do something practical about it. And the children sniffing glue. *And* the child beggars. A justice sent a whole clatter of them to gaol the other day to be kept in safe keeping till someone could decide what to do with them, and the governor of the gaol let them all out again immediately. He said he had no authority to keep them in, they being children.

ES: How could he keep them in, the darlings? Do you know what it costs to keep a child in that new children's reform place? A thousand pounds a week no less. Do you want to ruin the country having all these toddlers arrested just for sitting around on the pavements?)

Unfortunately there are more than toddlers involved. There is a powerful drug trafficking organisation in Dublin, and swiftly extending its influence through the country, dealing in all the popular drugs including heroin, and aiming not simply at teenagers, but also at children. Ten- and twelve-year-old children are approached by drug pushers in their school playgrounds, given free samples and, when they are hooked, are told they can have more as a commission on whatever they sell to fellow pupils. The whole trade is in the hands of four Dublin gangster families, well known to the guards. But knowledge is one thing and evidence is another, and the guards say they have no powers to do anything constructive about the problem. The minuscule size and Heath Robinson equipment of the Dublin Drug Squad is an indication of the government's degree of interest in the matter.

A summary of Dublin's drug problem was given in a recent Irish TV programme, *Today Tonight*. Brendan Glacken, reviewing the programme for the *Irish Times*, commented as follows:

> It was reckoned that there were some 4,000 heroin addicts on the streets of Dublin, each of whom needs anything from £30 to £200 daily to finance the addiction. Taking the average cost at a modest £50, each addict was seen to need about £18,000 annually; resulting in an income of approximately £75 million for the pushers. Who are the pushers? An 'extended family', we were told, a mafia whose members are widely known, who organise systematic delivery and payment, but who can rarely be caught in the act in a marketplace where heroin in minute 'doses' changes hands so easily.

Certainly in September 1982 the guards moved against one of the families. A senior member was arrested, along with several 'pushers', who took about as many precautions getting their supplies of heroin as if they were buying cigarettes. A Garda officer said, 'They were just pulling up in cars, going into the flat for their supplies, handing over their cash and coming out again in broad daylight.' Which was either sheer stupidity, or total contempt for the guards and the Drug Squad, based on past experience. But any police force is only as good as the government that pays its wages and provides its equipment, and if there is almost no political willingness to spend whatever it takes to break the drugs racket, there is an almost equal unwillingness to help addicts. Jervis Street Hospital's Drug Centre does wonders with limited facilities, and without it the situation would be even worse than it is. But no government has yet put drug abuse high on their list of priorities for public spending. There are votes in contraceptives and weird airports. There are none in drugs.

Nevertheless, it is good to be able to record that in October 1982 the then Minister of Health, Mr Woods, showed a willingness to do something about the plight of teenage glue-sniffers when he announced a grant of £150,000 'for the purchase of a house in Co. Wicklow where young girls sleeping rough and sniffing glue could be taken' (I quote from the *Irish Times* of 21 October). That is certainly something to be grateful for.

Unfortunately a question remains. The Minister says the girls '*could* be taken' – not '*would* be taken'. Will there be legislation that will empower the proper authorities to take the children to the new home, and *keep* them there? And if so, will keeping them there be of real value to the children? Will the care they receive there give them a fair chance of a decent adult life? These questions seem unjust, following on a generous decision by the Minister and his department. But between a minister's good intentions and the ultimate result there is often a wide gap, and nowhere more so than in Ireland. What more could the Minister do?

Several things. One would be to discover the parents of these and other similarly neglected children, and prosecute them for neglect. Another would be, not simply to prosecute them, but to attempt to teach them the basic necessities of child care and family life. This would mean more than telling them of the 'services available to them', which in effect boil down to money and free handouts. It would mean real guidance as to how to use the money and the handouts so that they are not wasted.

Would this mean interference in family life? A diminution of freedom? Yes, it would. But glue-sniffing is an interference in family life, and so is putting the infant glue-sniffers into a children's home, however well run. Having to drive on the left is a diminution of freedom. Having drunken, ignorant, brutal parents is a diminution of freedom. Some of the glue-sniffers' parents – and the parents of all Ireland's neglected children – may be beyond hope of salvage. But some may not. I should love to hear of a strong effort being made to find out and, if some can be salvaged, to hear that it was being attempted.

Teenage drugs. Teenage alcoholism. Teenage sex. Teenage violence. There are areas in Dublin where the guards prefer not to go, unless in force. There are large areas of Dublin where ordinary citizens prefer not to go at all after dark, and sometimes not even in daylight. a great many women – and old-age pensioners of both sexes – live in terror even in their own homes. Houses are broken into by gangsters, and the women raped as well as robbed. Dublin has become a dangerous city to live in.

A couple of recent newspaper articles ('recent' as I write this. The likelihood is that as you read it things will be worse) illustrate the situation in Dublin. Eugene McGloin in the *Sunday Tribune* gives a 'picture of visitors running the gauntlet of pick-pockets and car thieves on city streets'.

In twelve months up to last July, 200 Americans lost passports as a result of attacks on them here, and more than one hundred French suffered a similar fate in 1981.

Many others lose money and suffer damage to their cars, and because all cases may not be reported, no one can be sure of the full scale of the problem ...

A British consular spokesman said: 'A typical incident would be a car coming off the ferry, and the driver pulls up to read a map of Dublin and a brick comes through the windscreen ...'

The growth of the city's drug problem has also added to the menace with many of the incidents being carried out by people either under the influence of drugs or desperately needing cash for another fix. 'The glue-sniffers are involved here and the growth of the drug scene has added to the problem. Tourists are seen as easy marks by the glue-sniffers. They don't expect to be attacked by children on the main street in the city and tend to be shocked when it happens,' he said.

The second article was also in the *Sunday Tribune*. In it Tom McGurk described a Dublin working-class suburb.

The whole area is like a jungle. Burnt-out cars and vans, smashed fences and street-lights, the roadways littered with broken glass, stones and dog excrement. The gardai and the dogs climb into the vans and set off on a tour of the St Helen's Drive area. We follow at a safe distance. In the garda van headlights people can be seen moving back from gateways and street corners to the shelter of their own front doors. Dogs howl from distant darkened streets, lights come on and off.

We slow further behind, as the gardai had warned us that they were often ambushed. Usually the ambushes are launched from the small laneway beside The Barry House. Sometimes up to fifty youths (and some girls) dash out after the passing garda van, pelting it with bottles, stones and sticks. They then turn and disappear into the dark silhouette of laneways and houses. Sometimes petrol bombs are used, usually so unprofessionally that they are as much a threat to the thrower as to the gardai. The blue garda Toyota Hiace vans were never designed for this sort of guerrilla warfare. It must be like being stoned inside a biscuit tin.

There is no ambush and the gardai slip back to Finglas station to unload their prisoners and rest. We park in a side street. Suddenly a huge Ford Granada screeches past, stuffed to the windows with youths. The lights are on full and the horn is blowing. This is called the 'stolen-car derby'. The car circles the grassless traffic islands, skidding and bouncing dangerously. A dark group on a corner cheer and fists come out of the windows raised in salute. The Indians have commandeered a covered wagon. The car heads off into the vast prairies of Finglas South.

Midnight now and the drinkers are emerging from The Barry House. The mohicans, barred or too young to be served, have taken to drinking cider in the open. Suddenly the garda vans are back and the dogs. One drinker takes an intense interest in one of the dogs. He removes his coat and approaches it, matador-like. The dog's ears prick up and it looks puzzled. 'Go home now' say the gardai. The dog remains impassive. From the nearby darkness a shower of stones rise up. It's quickly into the vans and off. There are certain places pressmen are afraid to go. One of them is up dark alleyways in Finglas where gardai in helmets and batons chase young mohicans. They emerge exhausted ten minutes later 'mohicanless'.

Within an hour though, the estate is quiet. There is no doubt that the garda tactics were aggressive, purposeful and, it seemed successful – well, for that night anyway. Come Sunday night, 'Mick's butcher stall', one of the two remaining shops in the complex at St Helen's Drive, was up in flames. After forcing the shutters, and stealing £3,000 worth of meat, the premises were sprinkled with petrol and put to the torch. The mohicans retired into the dark of their nearby field to drink their cider and watch the fire. What they did with £3,000 worth of frozen meat must be left to the imagination.

On Monday the gardai were sufficiently worried by a rumour to speak to the press about it. The night time van-raids and dog attacks had been so effective that the mohicans had drawn up a hit-list of gardai and had attempted to hire a gun. Word had come to the gardai, presumably from those who sell fire-water and guns to the Indians. Shopkeepers say they have refused to join protection rackets for their premises and are now being systematically burnt out one by one. With garda overtime cutbacks, numbers may be on the mohicans' side.

None of all the foregoing was imaginable twenty or even ten years ago. But for thirteen years we have lived next door to highly glamorised violence in the North. Night after night our children have watched TV pictures of other children throwing rocks at soldiers, doing their best to set fire to armoured cars, building barricades of blazing buses in streets out of a film set for Armageddon.

An armalite rifle and a stick of gelignite have been seen as the badges of manhood. Killing soldiers and policemen has been seen as the height of human achievement. (No one in the Southern Establishment has *praised* these things, but no one has condemned them either, in the sort of terms that reach the minds of half-educated and totally uneducated children.)

Our whole attitude to the Northern misery has invited retribution, and retribution is coming, not from outraged Northerners, but from our own internal barbarians, to borrow Toynbee's phrase. We have not praised the IRA but we have not condemned them. Oh yes, we have forbidden their appearance on our TV screens and in radio interviews (with the odd result that we get our information about the Provos from the BBC and not our own television station), but we have not made it crystal clear, in words of four letters, that we hate and detest and condemn the murders that are being committed in the name of Ireland.

And again and again there is an undercurrent of approval of what is done. Never publicly expressed, but *there*. An approval that is beginning to crystallise on new class lines, to add to and confuse the old geographical divisions, in which Dublin opposed all kinds of Republican violence, and the South and West and North-West approved of it, or at least sympathised with it. Now, in spite of their earlier rejection of Marxism and politics, the Provos are being seen as a working-class movement, as the champions not only of Northern Catholics but of the working-class North and South, of the unemployed, the dispossessed. When, during the Hunger Strike campaigns, there was a riot outside the British Embassy in Ballsbridge, some of the rioters eventually retreated before the garda baton charges and fled through the middle-class respectability of Sandymount, down towards Ringsend.

As they got clear of the guards they began invading gardens and houses, demanding shelter or refreshments, or both. And to their unwilling and terrified hosts and hostesses they said menacingly, 'It'll be your bloody turn next. You're effing comfortable here in your effing little houses, but just you wait!'

With unemployment running as high or higher than England's and the guards already financially overstretched, we may not have to wait very long. We have been promised 2,000 extra guards (a promise made before and never kept), and by the time you read these words we may well have them. Although this week the government here has just decided in the name of economic realism to slash 8 million pounds from the Department of Justice's budget, which does not look promising for garda recruitment or equipment. Oddly enough, no one mentioned the possibility of saving the £8 million by cancelling Knock airport instead. But the real answer is not extra guards, or guards carrying arms, or granted extra powers – nor is it more prisons, nor harsher laws, nor longer sentences, nor hanging, nor the birch. A New York policeman once said that the police are standing at the far end of society's sewer pipe. All they can do is collect the dung in buckets and bury it, if they have enough buckets. They can do nothing about the smell. And if society doesn't like the smell it must change its diet.

Our diet in Ireland has become identical with England's, and America's, and that of the whole 'civilised' world – greed and violence. Greed is no longer one of the seven deadly sins, it is the first essential of success. The man with two motor cars and two houses, and a wife with two mink coats and diamonds, is a successful man, no matter how he got the things. As for the nightly diet of violence on TV, in fact and fiction; it would be hard to support the argument that this causes satiety in the viewer and leads to an interest in peace and quiet. And for a great many poor children this nightly slaughter is the only real education they will ever get – the slaughter, and the images of delightfully advertised luxuries they are never going to be able to afford, from sleek cars to sleek women.

If, when they grow old enough to be able to do anything about it, they pick up the nearest weapon and set out to take what they want by force, who is entitled to be surprised? Nor do they have to grow that old before they begin. Street gangs of ten- and twelve-year-olds are becoming commonplace, mugging women, robbing and burgling.

Another horrible commonplace of modern Ireland is rape. Ireland is such a small country, with such a small population, that any crime statistics sound ludicrously unimportant to a reader in London or New York. But first of all you must multiply them by twenty to get a British equivalent, and next you must contrast them with the figures of only a generation ago, when Ireland's moral climate was still that of a 19th-century English village. Moreover, the official figures have to be taken not with a grain of salt but a large dose of disbelief. Just as on closer investigation Ireland's suicide rate turns out to be at least three times as high as the government statistics claim, so do the figures for rape. (Frank Byrne, in the *Sunday Independent* of 27 July 1982, reported how a team from the Department of Psychiatry, Regional Hospital, Galway, analysed the post-mortem records of over 400 residents of Galway who had died in one recent year. The four pathologists and three psychiatrists working on the project concluded that twenty-two of the deaths must have have been suicides, yet only two had been so designated in coroners' reports.)

As regards rape, according to the published statistics rapes in the Republic of Ireland for the years 1979, 1980, and 1981 have averaged just under 50 a year, with indecent assault cases running at something over 100 a year, rising to 120 in 1981. But in the twelve months ending 28 February 1981, when officially there were less than 50 rape cases in the whole country, the Dublin Rape Crisis Centre alone dealt with 126 cases. The reason for the discrepancy is not – as it is in the case of suicides – official concealment, but official ignorance. The majority, perhaps the great majority, of women who suffer rape do not go to the guards to complain.

Either they are afraid of the treatment they will receive if they do, or they are too shocked to think of anything but crawling home and hiding, or they are afraid of the rapist's vengeance if they report him, or the rapist is their own husband, or even their own father, or someone else whom they dare not report for fear of family or neighbourhood scandal. For every reason for reporting a rape there can be two or three equally powerful reasons for not reporting it. One of those reasons is that Irish society still does not take rape seriously enough, if at all. The *Sunday Press* journalist Ginnie Kennealy quotes the Professor of Criminology at Trinity College, Dublin, Mary McAleese, as telling her that:

> Men in our society are still socialised in such a way that they consider violence an acceptable reaction when things go wrong. In fact they consider it manly to go and beat someone up if he has wronged them. Fathers set their sons a bad example on this score, making physical punishment a norm for their sons and

daughters alike – and in some cases hitting their wives as well. Is it any wonder that young men grow up considering that violence against women is a normal response?

Parents and teachers have simply got to work hard to change this attitude and see that the children in their care grow up with a proper respect for women. There's also the question of the relationship between the sexes in Ireland which is abysmally bad because segregated education, church taboos on sexuality, and the traditional separation between the sexes at most social events has led to a deep lack of understanding between the sexes – and part of not understanding a class or an individual is often that you despise them.

There are two things we have to get over in this country; the first is this tremendous inhibition that both the judiciary and the gardai seem to have about getting involved in a case where there is a personal relationship between attacker and victim. Judges in general are remarkably lenient if a defendant claims that he had a basically good relationship with a victim but just lost control on this occasion.

The other is the leniency our whole society displays where drink or drunkenness is involved in a crime. Drunkenness is widely regarded as a mitigating factor here, whereas in other countries it would make the offence even more reprehensible. How often do we hear a judge say: 'You had drink taken, so you weren't really in control' and passing a lenient or even a suspended sentence – in extreme cases even letting a man out on bail possibly to commit a similar offence again.

Our judiciary really needs to think a lot and educate themselves further about these questions, and hopefully this should lead to a change. Traditionally, the weight of our whole legal system has been for the protection of property, not of people. And it is certainly time this was changed.

And the statistics of all this misery? In 1981 there were almost 60 per cent more armed robberies than in 1980. Indictable offences increased by almost 23 per cent. Property stolen in 1981 was valued at some £20 million, instead of a 'mere' £14.6 million in 1980. Perhaps even more alarming was the fact that the detection rate for all crimes fell from 39.9 per cent in 1980 to 36.6 in 1981. Which tells one nothing. Rape is not a statistic. It is a woman who can't sleep at night and who is afraid to go out of doors, even in daylight. Robbery is not a rising percentage, it is someone's home violated, with shit on the carpet and things broken, and irreplaceable belongings gone. Crime is not a line of figures on a report, it is evil let loose in a small country that was almost unaware of this kind of evil until yesterday. And who let it loose? There are so many targets for accusation, from 'the North' to TV to lenient judges to over-crowded schools to parsimonious governments to public indifference, that it is hardly worth making a list. But who will chain it up again? Or will it go on getting worse and worse until the criminals take over, or we beg for a 'strong government' that will turn out worse than the criminals?

Drug offences also increased during 1981. Some 1,256 people were found to possess illegal drugs compared with 991 in 1980. And there were 1,204 seizures of drugs compared with 813 the previous year.

The statistics also reveal that the drug problem has become more serious outside Dublin. In 1980, nobody was charged with drug offences in the Garda divisions of Laois-Offaly, Mayo, Roscommon-Galway East and Sligo-Leitrim. Last year, however, forty-three people were charged with drug offences in these places. In Kerry, the number of drug offences jumped from fifteen in 1980 to thirty-five in 1981; in Limerick, there was a rise from three to forty-six; in Clare just one person was charged in 1980 but last year there were charges against thirty people. (These figures reflect an increase in drug crimes and usage rather than in the detection rate. Heroin abuse is now a major epidemic in Ireland, the figures being comparable to those of New York a few years ago.)

10 The 'Fair City'

Greater Dublin has a population of over a million, and ranges from the cocktail party elegances of Foxrock in the south, to the high rise horrors of Ballymun in the north, where the women live on tranquillisers and trudge up fifteen flights of stairs with a perambulator because the lifts have been vandalised yet again. (This north/south division between genteel and bleak extends right through Dublin, and indeed right through Ireland.) The north side of Dublin – long ago the 'Danish town', the 'Danes' having been expelled from the south side of the river where they built the first townlet – the north side, that became the fashionable side in the 18th century, full of Georgian houses and elegant squares and wide streets – town planning was first tried out on the Irish to see if it was dangerous – the north side declined right through the last hundred years to become a desert of neglect, slums, tenements, demolition sites and parking lots, a landscape only relieved by a couple of fine hotels and some cinemas. It now forms as horrid an entry to central Dublin from the airport as any city can offer.

The south side of Dublin, on the other hand, is full of genteel charm, small parks, pretty gardens; Dublin is a city of gardens, where it is still easy to imagine oneself in the country, surrounded by apple trees and birds. (Magpies are taking over, probably sent here by the English in revenge for Mr Haughey not supporting Mrs T. over the Falklands.) In recent years a brave effort has been made to revitalise the north side – not, I have to add, by any official body, but by various imaginative individuals (the name of Guinness ranking high among them) and two or three private companies. They have bought old tenements and turned them into private houses of immense dignity and, often, splendour. But these are isolated cases, the restored houses standing in a terrace of ruins, or flanked by other tenements or by nothing at all, shored up on either side by timber supports. (Georgian building, in Dublin anyway, was not always that sound. In a terrace each house relied on its neighbours to keep it upright. In some terraces the party walls were lined with turf sods, between skins of lath and plaster.)

Being isolated, these restored houses really do no more than underline the general decay, like one sound tooth in a mouth full of blackened stumps. Georgian architecture depended for its effects on wholeness, on a panoramic sweep of view along a terrace or around a crescent or square. Thanks to 20th-century indifference, that wholeness has gone for ever. The Corporation, which could have saved acres of Georgian Dublin, has preferred to demolish, and to shift the tenement dwellers out to frightful estates on the perimeter, like Finglas and Ballymun, Ballyfermot and Tallaght, where the general horrors of Corporation architecture and 'estate' planning – or lack of it – invite nervous breakdowns and vandalism. Thousands of city dwellers were exiled to such places, and arrived finding no shops, no pubs, no cinemas, no parks, no play schools, no community centres, no sports grounds and a large and hideous church. They were often lucky if the roads had been surfaced.

The Corporation – and the well-to-do – were subsequently astonished at the ingratitude of people given the chance to live in such lovely new houses. To make it worse, existing communities of city slum dwellers were usually broken up as a matter of policy, some being sent here, some there, so that not only did the arriving exiles find no 'amenities' – meaning nothing to do except to try to rob the local bank – but also no friends. And there was a fashion for sending all people of the same age to the same place, so that a new suburb might consist of 10,000 recently married couples, all with tiny children. The result was chaos.

The present Corporation now deeply regrets what its predecessors did, but cannot afford to correct their mistakes. It would love to pull down the Ballymun tower blocks, and thereby save at least a million pounds a year in losses, but it cannot begin to afford to rehouse the unhappy flat dwellers. And they *are* deeply unhappy. A recent television documentary described the conditions in the working-class suburb of Finglas, and set off a predictable row with Establishment Spokespeople shrieking that it was a dirty lie, and a slander on the fair name of decent, hardworking Irish people. The inhabitants of Finglas reacted either with eager acceptance of the 'slanders' or with total apathy, being presumably too stunned by their surroundings to care.

(ES: I'm listening to all of this and I'm not a bit happy with it. I never shrieked in my life. I'm well known for having a musical, attractive voice and when I sing harp accompaniments at small select soirées in Ballsbridge and Donnybrook I'm always highly complimented. You can change that lie about Spokespeople shrieking – put Spokes*persons*, the right word is '*persons*', 'people' sounds common, which is why you wrote it – put ... don't put anything about Spokespersons even. You're only doing it out of malice and sarcasm. Put 'Well informed circles contradicted the biased and distorted views of the crypto-Communist journalists and so-called investigators who produced a totally unrecognisable caricature of a typically hardworking, self-reliant, Irish community, full of initiative, charity, and piety, self-help, neighbourliness –

C: I'm putting it down word for word.

ES: You can also put down about our glorious public buildings. The Customs House –

C: Will I put down that some 19th-century eejit built a railway viaduct in front of it so that you can't see it properly? And will I tell them about the Cathedral and the Corporation building its new offices in front of *that*? And the Bank of Ireland's new building that someone said looks like a stranded oil rig? And the new university buildings out at Belfield – the ones like air-raid shelters that give the students claustrophobia and manic depression? And the new library in Trinity? I've told them about the American Embassy already, but I could tell them again. And Liberty Hall, that has a kind of little frill on top as if someone sat on it and it got squashed? And how they've gutted the whole of the north side and only God and the Corporation know what they've got in mind to put there, except that it will be unspeakable – and probably inhuman.

ES: You will not put down one of those things. Do you not realise that our tourist industry is vital to the economy of this country, and that tourists come to see our beautiful buildings and our beautiful countryside and that neither they nor we want some smart alec telling lies about them. It is a well known fact that American tourists are overwhelmed by the gracious tranquillity of our lovely capital. They stand in awe in front of St Patrick's Cathedral where Dean Swift wrote *Gulliver's Travels*. They stand speechless with wonder as they gaze at the majestic columns of the Bank of Ireland, and the noble facade of Trinity College, redolent of so much of Irish history – Grattan's Parliament, Wolfe Tone, the United Irishmen, Bold Robert Emmet, Edmund Burke whose noble statue accompanies that of charming Goldsmith on either side of the stately entrance to the College, through which a hundred generations of Irish students have flocked out into the wider world to spread the fame of Irish scholarship. The visiting American stands gazing at these wonderful buildings while a panorama of Irish history unfolds before his eyes. The Danes arriving a thousand years ago to tame the marshes of the Liffey and build the first Irish town – it not being the custom of Gaelic Ireland to dwell in towns, but rather to roam the untrammelled countryside, pursuing the noble stag and fierce wolf in merry hunting parties –

C: Excuse me –

ES: Yes?

C: If that American is standing there speechless it's not because of the panorama of Irish history, it's because he's just had his hotel bill. Americans are practical people. (A family of father, mother and two teenage children spending a week in a good Dublin hotel, with a double room and bath for the parents, and a single room each for the son and daughter, plus breakfast and service charge, will receive a bill for about £1,300. In an equivalent hotel in, say, Galway or Killarney, with half board, the bill would be about £600. For one week. The Irish Tourist Board is constantly amazed that Irish holiday-makers increasingly prefer the Costa Brava, and incoming tourists are becoming an endangered species. Incidentally, those relatively modest prices are for budget-conscious tourists. Business travellers who like to be looked after, and who get their accounts paid by their companies, will pay a lot more. Currently Ireland tops the Expense Account League for Europe, at £94 sterling per day for a visiting executive who wants first-class accommodation, reasonable meals, drinks and a hired car. Or for a well-to-do tourist who likes luxury. This compares to £84 for Britain and £52 for Luxembourg. By the time you read this, these prices will be history, due to inflation. But at a current inflation rate of at least 19 per cent per annum Ireland is not likely to have lost her place at the head of the list.)

ES: I knew you'd say something like that. You are not just a hack. You are a vulgar hack. But is even your ink-stained soul not brightened by the thought of Ancient Ireland? The Hill of Tara. Malachy and his collar of gold. The noble banqueting hall, the handsome warriors –

C: The skinheads in St Stephen's Green? And the punk rockers? The ones with their hair in spikes and dyed different colours?

ES: Be silent! 'Farewell Patrick Sarsfield wherever you may roam. You crossed the sea to France and left empty camps at home!' Oh Sarsfield, our hero! Our lost leader! Will ye no' come back again?

C: This chapter is about Dublin.

ES: Be quiet! Do you remember the Lament of the wife of Art O'Leary, who was killed by the Protestant scoundrel Morris for refusing to sell him his lovely mare for five pounds sterling, a curse on the Penal Laws and the devils who framed them? An Irishman and an officer and a gentleman of ancient lineage not allowed to own a horse worth more than five pounds!

C: Dublin is situated on the banks of the river Liffey, made famous by James Joyce as 'Anna Livia Plurabelle', and the English name of the lovely city derives from two Irish words, *Dubh*, meaning black, and *Linn* meaning a pool. So that it's the merest chance that Ireland's gracious capital is not called Blackpool. The Irish name for Dublin, on the other hand, derives from the fact that there was a ford across the river at this point, paved with hurdles made of sticks, and wattles, 'Baile Atha Cliath' meaning, approximately, the Town of the Ford of the Hurdles.

ES: Will you for pity's sake give over?

C: I will not. I am being honest and plain-spoken, uncontroversial, literary, highly educated, a credit to my country and to what was once the second city of the British Empire. I intend to proceed in this delightful vein for some time, describing how, in the 17th century, the wandering and marshy course of the Liffey was at last tamed and channelled by the system of stone quays that exists to this day and that made possible the reclamation of large tracts of land on which prosperous suburbs now stand, forgetful of their unstable and tidal past. I intend to tell them about the spread of the city's boundaries south-eastwards, turning what was once the haunt of duck and tern, not to mention drake and water-hen, into the idyllic precincts of that handsome park renowned the world over as St Stephen's Green. Where indeed ducks and other aquatic creatures still swim about on the tastefully designed lake, taking refuge at night on delightful islands set in the watery expanse for that sole purpose.

ES: Will you give over?

C: Why? In the glorious period at the end of the 18th century when Grattan's Parliament – so called, if a shade inaccurately, by our popular history books – when for the first time in our chequered history an Irish parliament held unchallenged sway over a united and peaceful Ireland, it seemed to many that Ireland's long frustrated dream of unity and nationhood and freedom had at last begun to be realised. All that was fair and noble in Irish society began to turn to Dublin as the centre of the universe. Magnates built mansions there of unparalleled elegance. Gentlemen of estate, noble ladies, great merchants, all who wished to have a voice in Irish affairs – and what patriot did not? – competed to build and furnish with the utmost dignity, nay, opulence, and artistic taste, the Georgian houses whose sad relics may still be seen in Mountjoy Square and Parnell Square and their environs. Experts in stucco work were brought from Italy for no other purpose than to decorate wonderfully proportioned ceilings that in later times looked down on the miserable hunger and wretched illnesses of 19th- and 20th-century tenement dwellers. All, all our fond hopes were dashed by the abject treachery of our elected representatives who, bribed by pensions and offices, titles and favours, voted to destroy our independence and accept Union with England.

ES: I'm sick of this, and more than sick of it. Do you not know one line of poetry? Not one elegant phrase? One Raithi Deasa?*

* A beautiful phrase, fit for quotation and repetition.

C: I was going to say that of course there were two views even about the Act of Union, and that the Catholic view was that it was a great smack in the eye for the Protestant landlords who had been running the Irish parliament and having things all their own way.

ES: You have no respect for anyone or anything. You're a muckraker. Your natural home is a gutter.

C: That phrase 'muck-raker' is widely misunderstood. It's all part of present-day ignorance. The original muck-rakers were a courageous band of crusading American journalists, determined to expose corruption even if they had to dig in mud and worse than mud to get at the truth. The term first appears in literature in *The Pilgrim's Progress*.

ES: I don't want to know that! I refuse to be told such things! Ireland is the Children of Lir, turned into swans by wicked enchantment. Ireland is Diarmuid and Grainne, as innocent as the dew on the grass. Ireland is an old man with a clay pipe, leaning on a stone wall in the west, his grey head filled with old stories and wisdom. Ireland is a bunch of shamrock on St Patrick's Day, symbol of the Blessed Trinity. Ireland is children playing hop-scotch in a sunny street. Ireland is a pint of Guinness on a hot day. Ireland is a herd of cattle knee-deep in rich grass. Ireland is a lamp set in a window of a lonely cottage on a mountainside in the darkness. Ireland is me.

C: Are you finished?

ES: No. Ireland is Grafton Street on a spring morning with the pretty girls in their new dresses, and the smell of fresh-roasted coffee from Bewley's Café. Ireland is a white road in Mayo with the wild flowers like coloured stars on the bog and the larks singing. Ireland is a bank of turf by the roadside and the water shining in the bog holes like brown ebony. Ireland is fresh butter and hot griddle cakes and strong tea and strawberry jam. Ireland is innocence. Ireland is passing the time of day with strangers. Ireland is saying 'God save you' and 'May God shorten the road for you'. Ireland is a ruined tower covered with ivy and the rooks cawing round its top. Ireland is the Ban Shee crying, and ghost stories by a turf fire. Ireland is a mist of rain from the West, and then a burst of sunlight to gladden your heart. Ireland is Brent geese coming in to rest on the slob lands, and swans on the Liffey, and puffins on the rock ledges of the Skelligs, and wrens in the hedges. Ireland is the gorse burning yellow and the broom golden and the heather a purple shadow. Ireland is turf like green velvet where the sheep have nibbled it. Ireland is –

C: This is making me quite sick. Ireland is rusty motor cars abandoned in beauty spots. Ireland is corrugated-iron roofs and rusty barbed wire and piles of rubbish in corners and discarded soft drink tins and ice cream wrappers and transistor radios and chain-saws and unsilenced motorbikes destroying the peace and quiet of the countryside and the lakes polluted and the rivers poisoned –

ES: You can stop right there and pack your bags. I'm holding the floor. This is a beautiful country full of hospitable people, with the exception of a few yobs and yahoos like the despicable author of this despicable book. If you decide to come to us there'll be a welcome on the mat and my sister in County Cork keeps a bed and breakfast place at very modest prices, furnished in the height of modern taste and elegance. You can get her address from Bord Failte or I'll send you her business card and rates on request. And Cleeve has not another living word to say about that or about anything else. This is definitely and unconditionally *the end*. Signed, ES.)

11 Final Thoughts

As Dr Johnson said, we are a fair people – we never speak well of one
another. (You may agree with ES that I am reinforcing this image
with every line I write. Alas, alas, it was never my intention.) I once
heard an American professor explain our begrudgingness in terms of
village life. 'Ireland is a national village,' she said, 'and in a village
there is usually only one of every desirable thing. If you've got it, I
can't have it. And I'd rather see nobody have it than you enjoying it
while I have to go without.' She went on to imply that city life was
different.

I was deeply impressed by this until I began to think of the literary
and artistic vendettas of London and Paris and New York – and of
Classical Athens and Renaissance Rome for that matter. The world is
full of begrudging villages, even in the middle of large cities. People
are people wherever they live, and the generous-spirited man who
loves to see his neighbours do better in life than he has done is a sad
rarity, in England and America as in Ireland. And when I am
tempted to claim that at least in our begrudgingness and our internal
feuds we display a Celtic ferocity and intensity that it is quite
remarkable, and almost an art in itself, I have to hesitate again, and
think of Corsicans, and Spaniards, and Parisians, and the
inhabitants of Bloomsbury, and Oxford dons, and the internal
quarrels of the BBC, and the machinations of the English Foreign
Office, and New York Society, and Bulgarian politics, and Albanian

politics, and the Kremlin, and Pekin, and the Gang of Four, and the English Labour Party – and I have to fall silent in awed amazement at the horrid nature of the world and the childlike innocence of Irish life, both private and public.

In Ireland we do not know the meaning of vengeance or intrigue. Our intriguers are infant amateurs, whether as politicians or writers or professors or lovers or diplomats. Noisy children. And the epithet 'noisy' is as much a key to our character as the words 'children' or 'amateurs'. We are tremendously noisy about everything we do, and everything we achieve or pretend we have achieved or like to think we have achieved. Together with the Jews, but perhaps with a shade less justification, we are the world's finest self-advertisers. Where other nations merely do things, we talk about having done them, with such conviction that the world takes the word for the deed.

We say we are famous lovers and the world believes us. We say we are mighty boozers, capable of drinking a barrel dry and then rushing out to fight six men and lay twelve virgins. And the world claps its hands in wonder, failing to notice the helpless, shivering alcoholic in the corner who has just made the boast. We say we have suffered more wrongs than any people in history, and the world, ignoring all reality, believes us, and weeps for us, and dyes its beer green on St Patrick's Day, and gives us money so that we can go and suffer more wrongs in the North of Ireland.

We say that we are an educated, cultured people whose very peasants used to quote Greek as they tended their sheep on the Kerry hills, and professors listen to us open-mouthed, waiting to hear wisdom, while vast numbers of our children leave school unable to read ten lines of a newspaper or write a legible application for a job.

I wish we were not famous for these things, because people come looking for them and reinforce our complacency. And when occasionally a visitor does not, but complains politely about some minor blemish, such as the filth of our streets and beaches, the astronomical price of our hotels and restaurants, our inhumanity in allowing half-naked children to beg in the winter streets, the sheer vandalism of our modern architecture and planning decisions, the way in which late-night revellers in a hotel or a private house are allowed to ruin everyone else's rest for half a mile around, our driving habits, the state of our roads, or anything else – then our

Establishment sets up such shrieks of outrage that one would imagine that the English Navy had captured Bantry Bay and that the Royal Air Force was bombing Dublin.

The pity of it is that all this horror and hullabaloo is unnecessary. We don't need to claim anything, because fundamentally, behind our obvious faults, we are indeed a pleasant, charming people. Visually illiterate we may be. Careless, untidy, unhygienic, given to ripping-off visitors if we have half a chance, noisy, dirty, drinking too much, unfair to women or, if we are women, spoiling our sons and putting up with murder from our husbands, we are the living image of almost everyone else on earth. We are as we are not because we are Irish, but because we are people.

And behind all our faults as people there is the charm of people. We are kind – if not always to each other – and friendly, if you give us half a chance, and easy-going even if that is another word for lazy. We still have time to talk to one another, and to you if you'd like to join in. We may be provincial and parochial and insular – and underneath the easy welcome we may be slow to accept strangers really into our lives (I know a labourer who has lived thirty years in his present village, but he is still an outsider, because he was born nineteen miles away), but we will give you a welcome, and welcome you back again as if we had been waiting for no one else the year long. In the way that Italians do. And you do, probably. And everyone else.

And we still have our Dr Bodkins (though maybe not our W.B. Yeatses) even if we still have our Beppos. We have beautiful horses, and stunningly beautiful girls, with skin like milk and eyes like the sky. We have Atlantic beaches that on a fine summer's day could shame Hawaii, although admittedly a fine summer's day in the West of Ireland is not an annual event. We have creamy Guinness and wonderful brown bread, if you know where to look for it. (If you don't know where to look for it you may find yourself stopped up with quick-setting cement.) We have gorgeous bacon and delicious sausages, and even free-range eggs here and there, which can provide the best breakfast this side of Paradise (although the hotel chains work on the principle that a really good sausage would be so unfamiliar to visitors that there's no point in providing them).

We have *The Book of Kells* and the Ardagh Chalice and the Rock of Cashel and the Irish Derby and the Ring of Kerry, and you might win £100,000 on the Irish Sweep. We have quiet places where even transistor radios have still not reached. We have people as nice as any you will meet in the whole wide world. But I would truly hesitate to claim that that niceness is due to being Irish. Perhaps it's simply due to being behind the times still, to not having *quite* caught up with the 1980s, and the rat-race, and the obligation to do the other fellow before he does you. Perhaps there is still a faint whiff of the 19th century and the 18th century about Ireland, in spite of the traffic jams and the Japanese factories. Long may it last.

Afterword

The government has just announced that Ireland is broke, and that next year will be worse. This is wonderful news – not that we are broke, which we all knew – but that the government has realised it. And not just any government but the Real Crowd. Wonders will never cease. Not only has the Real Crowd faced the facts of life, fearlessly, patriotically, stoically, Celticly, it has done something about it. No – not Knock airport. That's going ahead, thanks be to Heaven, another £2.7 million is being poured into the bog as these lines are written, and how could £2.7 million be better spent in a crisis than making it possible for Boeing 707s to land on top of a mountain in Mayo? No, Knock is safe. But, with ruthless economy, the Leader stepped in and stopped a junior class chieftain disguised as a junior minister going off to a far-flung conference, at a saving of no less than £25,000. I've calculated, with the aid of a small computer, that if 400 junior ministers don't go to conferences, it will just about pay for the Knock runways.

This was not the only good news in a wonderful week. Leaning over the quay wall by the Ha'penny Bridge (it was so called, in the unlikely event of your wanting to know, because there used to be a ha'penny toll to cross it. Before the bridge was built the only way to cross at that point was to be rowed over in a rowing boat, which cost a penny.) Anyway, there I was staring at the water, wondering if the above attack of government clearsightedness heralded the end of the world or just of the Real Crowd, when I saw fish swimming about in the murk below. Live fish! In the Liffey! In the middle of Dublin! Large ones! Admittedly a bit dingy looking, and swimming rather languidly, but beyond question alive and well, if temporarily insane. Either the fish are getting to like pollution, or so many factories along the river have gone bust that they're no longer doing their job of poisoning the environment.

Finally, really finally this time, as I walked back past the Shelbourne Hotel, I saw a girl sitting on the edge of a hole in the pavement mending a telephone cable. And not one single Mother of Ten went up to her to tell her she was a disgrace to Ireland, and not one single male chauvinist stopped to kick her into the hole to teach her her proper place in society. It *is* the end of the world.

Or at least the end of this book, leaving space only for a final apology for my insanity in having attempted to write it, and in imagining even for a moment that anyone, let alone myself, could achieve a fair likeness of Ireland in a book of a few chapters, or even a library of books. Have I come even near a reasonable caricature, or the simplest cartoon sketch of this complex and bewildering country? It is not for me to say yes to either question, and I can safely leave it to others to say no to both. As I write these last lines of a book already too long I can think of a thousand things I could have included and perhaps should have. How beautiful Ireland still is, for example, and how kind her people are, give or take a few monsters. How pleasant life can be, for those above the most abject poverty line. How little the rat-race mentality has affected us here, even in Dublin, in comparison with the rest of the 'civilised' world.

Have you ever had the experience of driving along an auto route, caught up in the frenzy of the traffic? Determined that no one should pass you, if your engine should explode with the effort? Determined to get somewhere before some essential moment? To drive farther, to drive faster, than ever before? To go. To go. To go. To go. And then for some reason, exhaustion, or a return to sanity, you pull into a picnic area, find a place, and switch off the engine. And get out and walk deeper among the trees.

The cataract roar of the traffic fades behind you. You can hear birds singing, insects, your own footsteps in the fallen leaves. The sun is on your face, and there are cows in the field. There are small white clouds in a summer sky. You can breathe deep without feeling poisoned. You can stand still and think without getting run over. And the traffic noise in the distance seems like the insanity that it is. What on earth have you been doing? Why? Why haven't you been spending the whole day like this? Why go back?

There is a wire fence surrounding the picnic ground but there is a gate in it, and beyond the gate a path leads into a wood. You open the gate, and follow the path, and in five minutes you are in another world. The world as it ought to be. And you feel a tightening at your heart because in a few more minutes you are going to have to go back to the picnic ground with its picnic litter. And your motor car. And the auto route. And the petrol and diesel fumes. And the madness. Why not stay for ever in the silent wood? Surely around the corner there must be a cottage to let, with an apple orchard, and a pond for ducks and geese, and hens pecking corn, and a view across the hills? Why not stay for ever?

That is Ireland. Many people have come here for a holiday and are still here, ten and twenty and thirty years later. Their actions speak much louder than any words. Certainly than any of mine.

THE END

Irish Words in English

The Irish language has contributed many things to English, via Anglo-Irish literature, but its direct contribution by means of words adopted into English from Irish seems very small – a surprising poverty, given the long history of Irish immigration into England. But such borrowings or adoptions of Irish words as do exist are often surprising to the non-specialist.

'Bother' is one, which Professor T.F. O'Rahilly suggests could be derived from middle Irish *Bódhar*, meaning deaf, before 1300, when the Irish pronunciation would give the appropriate form in English. Bother has subsequently come to carry such a wide range of meaning that 'deaf' seems inappropriate, but the earliest English meaning is 'noise', and of the verb to bother, 'to bewilder with noise'.

A more obvious borrowing is 'shamrock', from Irish *seamróg*, adopted into English in the 16th century, along with '*brogue*' for a shoe. In the 17th century there are 'leprechaun' (from Middle Irish *luchrupán*), 'Ogham' (the early Irish runic alphabet), 'Tory' (from Irish *Tóraidhe*, a pursuer and, by a paradoxical development, an outlaw, one who is pursued). 'Tory' appears as the name of an English political party in 1689, at the same moment that the Dutch Protestant marching song 'Lilliburlero' was becoming known in Ireland as the battle song of William of Orange's men. Later it was adopted by the Catholic armies and supporters, much as 'Lili Marlene' was adopted by the English and their allies from the

Germans in the Second World War. Also in the 17th century there is 'galore' (Irish, *go leór*, meaning enough), 'rapparee' (originally simply an Irish pikeman, but in contemptuous usage a bandit).

In the next century there are 'banshee' (*bean sídhe*, a fairy woman, but of a sinister kind, one who signals the death of those who hear her cries). There is 'shillelagh' (from the name of the woods in Co. Wicklow from which much-prized oak clubs were supposed to come), 'spalpeen' (*spailpín*, a labourer) and one or two others that are no longer used in English, such as 'planxty,' a harp tune, and 'pollan', a lake, along with 'fiorin', a kind of coarse grass.

In the 19th century there are 'blarney', from Blarney Castle in Cork whose battlements house the famous Stone, needing to be kissed by anyone who wishes to possess the gift – a right piece of tourist nonsense. There is 'colleen' (from Irish *cailín*, a girl), 'keen', (Irish *caoine*, a lament), 'carrageen' (from the place name, where a type of seaweed-cum-moss was and still is exploited as a valuable food and source of iodine). And there is 'crannog', a word adopted by 19th-century archaeologists to describe Bronze or Iron Age lake dwellings, first in Ireland or Scotland and later wherever they occur in Europe.

There are also words of disputed origin such as 'shanty', which could, and one feels may, have come into English from *sean-tigh*, meaning perhaps an old house, or more probably a public house of the poorer sort. But the weight of authority inclines to a French derivation from Canadian-French *chantier*, a woodcutters' headquarters. And there is 'phoney', from the Irish *fáinne*, a ring. (Apparently Irish emigrants to New York sold brass rings on street corners, claiming them to be gold, and calling them *fáinnes*, so that *fáinne* soon became a synonym for fake. It is still an Irish custom to put a brass ring in a cake on Hallow's Eve, its finder being supposed to obtain a husband or wife in the coming year. The emigrants who sold rings in New York may easily have got the idea from these 'barm brack rings', which of course imitated gold wedding rings.)

Another odd borrowing is 'pet', from Old Irish *peata*.

And perhaps the most surprising borrowing is not from Irish at all, but from Anglo-Irish – the word 'unwell', never known in English until imported by Dean Swift in the 1730s. Other Anglo-Irish words that have found a place in everyday English are 'hugger-mugger', 'crawthumper', 'smithereens', 'Come all ye' (as a generic term for a ballad or dancing song), and a few more like them, some of them confined to particular districts like Glasgow or Liverpool where there has been a large Irish population for centuries, or to some particular patois, like London thieves' slang, or beggars' cant. Even more obscure borrowings come from the tinkers' language, Sheldru, for which please look to Appendix B.

A very late and not quite linguistic borrowing in English from Irish is 'hooligan', taken not from the language, but the name of an Irish family in London in the 1890s, the Houlihans. The usage explains the derivation. Then from much earlier, at least the 16th century, there is 'cant', like 'keen' from Irish *caointe*, speech, and 'kern' and 'lough' from the 15th, neither of these latter now considered as part of everyday English speech. Many other apparently Irish words, such as 'hullabaloo', are from Scots rather than Irish Gaelic. Even bog is from Scots Gaelic *bogach*, although whiskey or whisky, claimed as Scots, should surely be regarded as originally Irish, *uisce beatha*, 'water of life', rather than Scots *uisge beatha* with the same meaning, but a *g* for Irish *c* in *uisce*. Another word often attributed to Scots rather than Irish Gaelic is 'gallowglass' (or 'galloglass'), a soldier or armed retainer of a chief in ancient Ireland and other Gaelic countries, from *gall*, a foreigner, and *óglach* a warrior (among other meanings).

But however hard one searches for Irish words in English, the list remains short. The only other word that springs easily to mind is 'shebeen', a low public house, but like hooligan this is not a pure linguistic borrowing, or if it is the original has yet to be traced.

APPENDIX B

The Tinkers and their Language

Often called 'Shelta', but properly called 'Sheldru', the language was never written down by the tinkers themselves, they being illiterate, but written records of it, of a desultory kind, exist from as early as the beginning of the 19th century. In the 1930s the Irish archaeologist R.A.S. MacAlister gathered up as many of these records as he could and compiled a Sheldru vocabulary and grammar. He appears to have done no field research – that was not to his purpose in a book devoted mainly to other things – but the present writer tried out MacAlister's vocabulary on tinkers in the late 1960s and found a complete agreement as to meanings. Here and there words had been lost. Today's tinkers no longer count in Sheldru, for example, and they have abandoned Sheldru 'given' names for conventional Irish ones. But apart from a sad, if natural, decay – paralleled, as I have said, in the decay of spoken Irish – the tinkers I questioned were capable of speaking a language that their ancestors of a hundred and fifty years ago had known and used.

And MacAlister suggests that the language is not merely a few centuries old, but in its origins is several thousand years old, representing the last remnant, however much distorted and altered, of a pre-Celtic language, onto which has been grafted very large additions drawn from Gaelic and other sources. His book *The Secret Languages of Ireland* (CUP, 1937), consists of examinations of five 'cants' or jargons in use in Ireland at one time or another; Ogham, used for inscriptions in pre-Christian and early Christian Ireland; Hisperic, a kind of secret scholars' language, used in the early Middle Ages in two forms, one based on Irish and the other on Latin; Bog-Latin, apparently the same type of dialect; Sheldru, with which this appendix is concerned; and Bearlagair na Saer, 'the masons' language', based on Irish and used by craftsmen in the later Middle Ages and for long afterwards.

There are connections between some of these dialects, and MacAlister suggests that underlying, or at least contributing, to some of them there is what he calls a 'serf-speech', an aboriginal, pre-Gaelic language spoken by outcasts and vagabonds long after Gaelic had become the language of the general population. Even if only a minute fragment of this pre-Gaelic speech survives in Sheldru it gives the language an immense 'archaeological' significance, and might make it possible to discover affinities elsewhere in Europe or North Africa or the Near East. A comparison with the handful of non-Celtic words in Irish might yield interesting results.

As for Sheldru words finding their way into English, there seem to be very few, as one would expect. The tinkers who brought the language to English-speaking areas of Ireland, or to England, did not move in respectable circles. If their language had an effect in England it would be on other jargons, beggars' or thieves'. In return, there is some Romani and also some East End of London slang in Sheldru, carried back to Ireland by returning migrants. The only words I have found that seem to have passed into general English usage are 'gammon', for deceitful talk, and 'game' for lame as in game-leg, both from Sheldru *g'ami*, meaning bad. In English slang there is 'ken' for a house as in drinking-ken, boozing-tan, ken etc. Eric Partridge in his *Dictionary of Historical Slang* looks to Romani *tan* and Hindustani *khan* for the derivation of 'ken', but both seem wildly unsatisfactory on various grounds. Sheldru *k'en* seems perfectly satisfactory as an explanation. There is also *pek* for food, which Partridge suggests comes from Welsh gypsy *pek*, to bake or roast. But Irish Sheldru *pek*, meaning bread, seems a better option, and the likeliest source for the Welsh gypsy usage. 'Stretch' in Sheldru means a year, and so it does in English prison slang, where 'carpet' signifies a three-month and 'pearl' a one-month sentence. There is no certainty that English thieves adopted the Sheldru word, but no one has offered a better explanation, unless of course the Sheldru word is a borrowing from the English slang. But this still leaves the origin unknown. Finally, at least by my reckoning, there is *tober*, a road, passing into 18th-century English as 'toby', the highway, and its derivations, such as a 'tobyman' (a highwayman), to 'toby' (to rob on the highway), 'high toby' (the same sort of thing done on horseback), whereas, as Partridge says, the footpad was guilty of 'low toby'.

APPENDIX C

Censorship

If one wished to gain some insight into the mental state of the Irish Establishment between the two world wars, one of the easiest and best ways would be to examine the list of books banned by the Censorship Board. The following titles and their authors are drawn from the list of banned publications for the year 1938. It includes most of the major writers of the period, and many of the great books. There is *To Have and Have not*, by Ernest Hemingway; *Turning Wheels* by Stuart Cloete; *Of Time and the River* by Thomas Wolfe; *Castle Corner* by Joyce Carey; *It's a Battlefield* by Graham Greene; *Pity for Women* by Henri de Montherlant; *Uncharted Seas* by Denis Wheatley; *Wheel of Fortune* by Alberto Moravia; *The Mother* by Sholem Asch; *The Song of the World* by Jean Giono; *Night and the City* by Gerald Kersh; *Women Must Work*, by Richard Aldington; *Fade-out* by Naomi Jacob; *The Dandy* by Laurence Meynell; *The Crusader's Key* by Eric Linklater; *Fontamara* by Ignazio Silone; *Selected Modern Stories* by H.E. Bates and others; *Self* by Beverley Nichols; *Tamarisk* by Netta Muskett; *Nightingale Wood* by Stella Gibbons; *Stamboul Train* by Graham Greene; *Country Tales* by H.E. Bates; *Don John's Mountain Home* by Ernest Raymond, and so on and so on.

Two years earlier, among many other books brought to the censor's notice, *The Painted Veil* by Somerset Maugham was banned, along with *Career* by Vicki Baum and *Bird Alone* by Sean O

Faolain. And it would be hard to think of any well known writer of
the thirties, forties and fifties some of whose books were not banned.
As late as 1966 the axe was still being wielded with puritan ferocity.
Four publishers in that year appealed against the banning of books
by their authors, among them Jonathan Cape, appealing on behalf of
August Is a Wicked Month by Edna O'Brien, and McGibbon and
Kee appealing on behalf of *Up the Junction* by Nell Dunn. Both
appeals were rejected.

Two years later things changed considerably, as if the wave of
revolt sweeping Europe in 1968 reached even the Censorship Board,
or its political masters. The personnel changed. More important, so
did the policy. From 1968 onwards writers such as Somerset
Maugham, or his latter-day equivalent, were safe enough. But even
in the seventies one could find authors on the list whose names seem
out of place beside *Bondage Quarterly, Discipline School, Lesbiana*
and *Teenage Spankers*. If it is necessary to protect Irish readers from
Forbidden Fruit, Famous Sex Comics and *The Sex Maniac's Diary*,
was it also necessary to protect them from Gore Vidal (*The City and
the Pillar*), Mickey Spillane (*The Erection Set*), Erica Jong (*Fear of
Flying*), Jean Genet (*Funeral Rites*), Leslie Thomas (*The Man with
the Power*), William Burroughs (*The Naked Lunch*), again, or still,
Alberto Moravia (*The Two of Us*), Robin Maugham (*The Wrong
People* – I obviously wrote too quickly about uncle Somerset and his
latter-day equivalents) and finally, joyous thought, Mary Whitehouse
(*The Mary Whitehouse Story*) _ No no no! Not *the* Mary W –? No, it
wasn't.

But looking through these wastelands of shame a strange fact
emerges. Certain writers seem to write dozens and dozens of books
each year and every one of then gets banned in Ireland. Timothy
Lea, for example (*Confessions from a Hotel, from the Clink, of a
Film Extra, of a Long-Distance Lorry Driver, of a Private Soldier, of
a Travelling Salesman* – a sequence broken by intruders, such as
Saspti Brata who copycatted with *Confessions of an Indian Woman
Eater* and Anonymous who provided *Confessions of a Sex Maniac*).
And the charmingly named Miss Tuppy Owens (the Miss is included
in the official list by some old-fashioned quirk of chivalry – by her
publishers? The censors?). She had eight titles banned between
March, 1974 and December, 1975 (all right, I admit eight in

twenty-two months isn't dozens every year, but it is a lot, isn't it? And for a girl, all by herself in a bed-sitter with a typewriter? Or in a luxurious Park Lane Pad, with three secretaries taking dictation? It's still a lot. And all banned! *The Summer Holiday Sex Manual, Sexual Paradise, Sexual Harmony, The International Sex Maniac's Desk Diary* – who *is* Miss Tuppy Owens? Could I meet her? (I feel we might have things in common.)

Is all this censorship necessary? Still? Does the Irish public of the 1980s need protection from Miss Tuppy Owens? And Timothy Lea? And Orrie Hitt? (*Dirt Farm, Call Me Bad, Nude Model*)? Would society come to bits if I had *The Sex Maniac's Desk Diary* for my appointments instead of the one my dog ate in a fit of boredom the other day? Would the appointments suffer? (Would my dog have suffered? The Dataday did him no harm at all.) Maybe. Maybe Ireland is a better, cleaner country for not reading *Girlie Fun, No.2*, or the *Tourist London Sex Guide*, or the *Randy Young Runaway*. I suppose it must be. But when one reads the rape cases that get into the papers (and most of them don't) one wonders if *The Joy of Sex in Colour* or *Sexual Harmony in a Motor Car* would make all that much difference.

(Looking at the most recent list of banned publications to come my way, dated April 1982, I'm sad to see no entry for Miss Owens. But there is a Miss Alice Masters, with an innocently titled volume, *The Adoption*. What horrors can that conceal within its covers? Is the name of the publishers, Swish Publications Ltd, a clue? And is Miss Alice Masters a pen name for Miss Tuppy Owens, attempting by this transparent subterfuge to sneak her work past the gimlet-eyed guardians of our morality? I wonder. I hate to think of Miss Owens abandoning her life's work in a sense of frustration at Ireland's lack of welcome. We would welcome you, we really would, if only we were allowed to.)

Books on Ireland

As well as the few Irish classics mentioned in the text of this book, anyone wishing to understand something about Gaelic Ireland should find the following of both value and interest. The choice is not quite as random as it might seem, being based on the suggestions of one of the leading Irish cultural and language organisations, Gael Linn.

The Hidden Ireland, by Daniel Corkery, a study of Gaelic-speaking Munster in the 18th century.

The Great Silence, by Seán de Fréine, an analysis of the decline of the Irish language in the 19th century.

The Love Songs of Connacht, by Douglas Hyde, the title explaining the contents.

The Poor Mouth, by Flann O'Brien, a satire on the culture and language movement of the past generation.

An Irish Navvy, by Dónall MacAmhlaigh, translated by Valentin Iremonger, being the diary of an Irish exile in England.

The Road to Bright City, by Máirtín Ó Cadhain, translated by Eoghan Ó Tuairisc, being a collection of short stories by one of the greatest, if not the greatest, of modern writers in Irish.

The Irish Language, by David Greene, a booklet published for the Cultural Relations Committee of Ireland at the Three Candles Ltd, a small publisher in Dublin, in 1966. Despite its small compass it gives a valuable survey of Irish life and culture, past and present.

This very short list of books could obviously be extended to far greater length, and any lover of Irish literature past and present will be indignant at so brief and arbitrary a selection. But to offer too many titles would, it seems to me, merely put off the newcomer to Irish culture, with the feeling that he or she could not possibly find the time for so much extra reading. And if the above books fail to kindle interest, no others are likely to succeed. While if they do, the new-found interest will soon lead to the discovery of more riches in Irish literature, without need of help from me.

APPENDIX E

Irish at Work

The Irish have two contradictory images as workers, as they do in so many other fields. On the one hand the world sees the Irish workman as drunkenly or charmingly work-shy, lying abed of a summer's morning, taking the afternoon off to go fishing and spending the evening drinking, in anticipation of not getting up to go to work tomorrow. If – this image suggests – the Irishman ever does get to work, he makes a delightful or maddening mess of it, fitting a rubber at each end of a pencil, putting the mug handle inside the mug so it won't get broken, and so on.

The other image of the Irish worker is the burly navvy (short for navigator, as 18th-century canal workers were termed, when Irish immigrant labourers helped to dig Britain's canal network), the tough and tireless hod-carrier or hole-digger, without whom Britain's road system, airports and houses could never have been built. Drunken he might be, but work-shy he is not, outlasting his frailer English and Scottish and Welsh rivals as cart horses outlast ponies when hitched to the plough.

(An ill-natured Irishman might turn round and say that in a period when it takes four Englishmen to do what one Japanese worker can do on his ear, it ill behoves the English to throw stones at the Irish as workers. But no Irishman would be so rude as to say anything of the kind.)

However, from an employer's point of view there are certainly things to be criticised about Irish attitudes to work. According to a recent survey we lose twice as many working days per year as does Britain – about 12 per cent of all working days are not worked in Ireland, which is an obviously unsatisfactory state of affairs, and we claim more and receive more per head in sick benefit payments than do workers in Britain. A reasonable guess would be that at least some of those sick benefits are related to hangovers rather than to calluses.

One factor in our attitude to work stems from our tax system and unemployment benefit payments, which manage to contrive that a married man with two children needs to earn £11,500 a year before he is better off at work than on the dole. Don't ask me how this is arrived at. I only wish I was on the dole. But to quote the Confederation of Irish Industry:

> ... In recent years there has been a decline in the relative reward for working. Persons receiving short-term welfare benefits, for example, are not subject to income tax, and this means that the money they receive while sick is greater than their net after-tax pay if they were working. This encourages absenteeism, and abuse of the system and probably stimulates the black economy.

As 'Maynard' of the *Sunday Press* goes on to explain, discussing the CII report:

> It can happen, also, that persons on a three-day week can have a higher disposable income than those working a full five-day week. Eligibility for short-term benefit was recently extended by the Dáil to those involved in certain trade disputes. The long-term unemployed on the other hand, cannot receive more than 85% of their net earnings, after deduction of income tax and PRSI. [Pay Related Social Insurance]
> The contrast with those receiving short-term benefits is startling. A person earning £7,000 a year has a gross wage of £135 a week, which, for a married man with two children, leaves him with a net take-home pay of £114. If he were receiving disability benefit, he would also get a pay-related benefit and a tax rebate, leaving him with £146, which is not

only more than his gross pay, but is 28% more than his net working pay. (He also saves on the cost of going to work, and so on.) A person is better off not working until his income is above £11,500 a year.

There is also another factor that needs consideration – the Catholic influence. Protestants believe in work as the road to Heaven; Catholics believe in Faith. This is half a joke and wholly an over-simplification, but it does reflect two almost opposite attitudes to work. The Englishman who doesn't work knows in his heart of hearts that he *ought* to work. The Irishman doesn't see why he should. There are other, far pleasanter things to do, and from a Catholic point of view – oddly enough – doing pleasant things is not always a sin, whereas from the Protestant point of view it is. So that the Irish workman in the German-owned factory who takes the day off to go shooting snipe feels that God won't mind. The German foreman expects God to strike the truant dead, and blames it on the Irish climate that God doesn't do it (God can't see him because of the mist that does be on the bog).

In sharp contrast to this general state of happy-go-lucky indifference to hard work, returned emigrants with experience of the tough world abroad often work extremely hard and build up large fortunes, to the jealous amazement of the stay-at-homes. As in all else, there is no generalisation one can make about Irish attitudes to work that the next anecdote one hears will not contradict.

The following story, reported in the *Sunday Press* in June 1983, may strike you as being typically Irish. But I wonder if stories like it occur elsewhere?

Social Welfare investigators have uncovered a huge 'black economy' racket operating right under the nose of officialdom. The racket was unmasked in a massive swoop on the forests of Wicklow where hundreds of timber harvesters were earning up to £300 a week on the 'lump' – and drawing the dole for good measure.

The crackdown led by the social welfare men with assistance from local foresters and gardai, had some extraordinary results. One sub-contractor hid up a tree for hours, afraid to come down until dark. Another lay in a drain covered with branches. Many escaped into the hills. Meantime, some of the city dwellers from social welfare got lost in the vast forests and had to be rescued by search parties.

But overall, the raid – described by one tax expert as 'the biggest manhunt in Wicklow since the escape of Red Hugh O'Donnell' – was a spectacular success. Even the most experienced sleuths were startled at the results.

Most of the timber harvesters, who number about 500, were drawing the dole in Ashford, Rathdrum, Blessington, Avoca and other Wicklow villages. Some of them were earning £300 a week tax free in addition to their dole payments.

An extraordinary aspect of the raid is that it took place several weeks ago, but none of the parties involved has publicised it. There are several reasons for this. The Social Welfare investigation squad are delighted – but the results are a severe embarrassment for the revenue commissioners. The harvesters are employed by private timber merchants whose accounts are seen by the revenue. Adding to the embarrassment is that an army of men were working untaxed on State land only 30 miles from Dublin, and drawing the dole simultaneously.

Irish Marxism

The modern Irish Establishment has never been happy about the strong Marxist element in the Revolutionary movement just prior to 1916, nor about its later survival as an undertone in more recent Irish history. Consequently little mention is ever made in popular accounts of the revolutionary struggle of the Irish soviets, the first to be established outside of Russia (although of briefer duration than those in Germany and Hungary).

In April 1919 a general strike was called in Limerick, following the shooting in hospital by British soldiers of an Irish prisoner who had been on hunger strike, Robert J. Byrnes, a member of the Trades and Labour Council of the Limerick Labour Movement, and also adjutant of the 2nd Battalion of the Limerick Brigade of the IRA. The following is an extract from *The First Dáil*, by Maire Comerford (published by Joe Clarke, Dublin, 1969):

> *LIMERICK STRIKE*: On Monday, April 14th, there began in Limerick City a strike protest against military tyranny which, because of its dramatic suddenness, its completeness, and the proof it offered that workers' control signified perfect order, excited world attention.
>
> Your committee were informed by telegram that a general strike had occurred as a protest against the 'Military permit' system ... A local volunteer had been shot ... At the funeral

British troops lined the roads with bayonets fixed, armoured cars passed the procession to and fro. Aeroplanes hovered over the hearse ... the people declined to be provoked.

Thereupon followed the proclamation of Limerick City as a special military area. In defining the boundaries the city was cut in two ... the effect of the proclamation was ... all workers (crossing the Shannon) had to obtain a military permit to proceed to and from their work and undergo examination at the bridge four times a day, by military sentries attended by policemen.

With the prospect that such conditions were to come into force on the Tuesday morning hurried meetings of the Trades Council were held on Sunday ... and it was decided to call on the whole of the workers of the city to cease work on Monday morning as the most effective form of protest available to them as Trade Unionists ... No work was done except by permission of the Committee. Shops were allowed to open for stated periods – scales of prices were fixed – food supplies were organised ... the city was policed by the Strike patrols. Your committee instructed Mr Johnson to proceed to Limerick ... to assist in every way possible the local committee.

The National Executive ... held meetings in Limerick ... An appeal was made for funds.

The Labour involvement had, in fact, been started much earlier; on 1 February the Limerick Trade and Labour Council, representing thirty-five unions, protested against the treatment of political prisoners in Limerick Jail and issued their own leaflet.

The strike was decided upon at 11.30 pm on the Sunday, but even so by Monday morning the Committee had a printed Proclamation displayed in the city: 'There was as much "sedition" printed in one hour during the strike as would normally get the operators ten years' imprisonment'. Money was printed, together with permits, lists of food prices, and a citizens' Bulletin. The Bishop of Limerick signed a manifesto, together with the principal clerics associated with his diocese. It protested not against the IRA, not against Labour, but against the British measures.

Unfortunately for the strikers, the bishop changed his mind, or had it changed for him, and in concert with the Protestant bishop he put it to the strike leaders that what they were doing was against the wider interests of the Irish people. When the Dublin-based railway unions refused to back the strike, the end was inevitable. The strikers lost, and the socialist element in the revolutionary struggle was driven still further into the background.

But the idea of a Marxist republic survived. To quote from another history of the period, *A History of the Irish Working Class*, by R. Berresford Ellis (Gollancz, London, 1972):

The workers were also growing in militancy during this period. During the spring of 1920 some fifty workers struck work at a creamery in Knocklong owned by Sir Thomas Cleeves, a prominent Unionist [properly Cleeve, not Cleeves, and the owner was Sir Thomas's son Frank, not Sir Thomas, by then several years dead]. The creamery was a trading centre for all the farms of the district and was a distributing centre of the towns – one of the biggest in Ireland. The dispute was over a question of wages. In May that year, the strikers, members of the ITGWU, decided to seize control of the factory under the slogan: 'We make butter, not profits!' and carry on the work in the factory and mill as the Knocklong Soviet Creamery. The farmers continued to supply milk to the creamery which continued to process and distribute. In May of the following year the Arigna coal mines in Co. Leitrim were also taken over by the workers and a red flag hoisted; in September, the port of Cork was taken over and run as a soviet; lands were seized by workers and run as communes or soviets, especially around Toorahara and Kilfenora, Co. Clare. Unlike their comrades in the north and midlands, the Munster IRA did not interfere with the confiscation of ranches and estates. In 1922 soviets were established in Mallow, Cashel and Ballingarry. The Labour Movement was highly embarrassed at the workers' radicalism, although Thomas Johnson, reporting to the Dublin Trades Congress in 1921, said that the establishment of Irish soviets was:

' ... the most important question that could be raised in the Labour Movement or in Social Economy ... It is a challenge, and let us make no mistake about it, to the rights of property. It says: though you happen to have a parchment which allots to you the right to use or possess this machine or that particular factory, though you have that power under legal enactment, henceforth that is not enough. We, as responsible to the workers, say these material things shall be continued in use so long as the community requires the product. That is the last issue raised and it is a contention that the Labour Party in Ireland, I hope, will continue to espouse and put into operation.'

But Labour declined to accept responsibility for the soviets. The Limerick and Tipperary soviets were destroyed by a boycott organised by the Irish Farmers' Union, a group of big ranch owners and farmers, while in Clare the soviets were reduced by farmers' units under military directions. The Knocklong Soviet Creamery was destroyed by English troops on August 22 as part of a systematic attack on Irish industrial life and especially co-operative creameries, mills and bacon factories. By April, 1921, English troops had destroyed sixty-one co-operative creameries alone.

The Irish in the First World War

At least 300,000 Irishmen volunteered for the British forces between 1914 and 1918, proportionately as many Catholics as Protestants, as many from the nationalist South as from the unionist North. Irish statistics for the First World War are difficult and confusing, in part because so many Irishmen emigrated in the years before the war, and joined the forces in England, or Scotland, or Wales, or the Dominions. whether they were then registered as Irish-born or, on being killed, were listed as Irish, was often a matter of chance. A second problem was the failure of many relatives in Ireland to inform the British authorities of the death of a son or brother or father on active service. Two further complications are the fact that many Irish recruits joined non-Irish regiments, or arms of the service, such as the Royal Artillery. And many so-called 'Irish' regiments, such as those raised in Liverpool or London, had large numbers of recruits who were not Irish. Accordingly all estimates both of general Irish recruitment and of Irish fatalities are liable to a wide margin of error.

Until recently the received wisdom was that about 500,000 Irishmen, from all parts of Ireland, joined up, and that about 50,000 were killed. Something over 49,000 names appear on the list of Irish war dead for the First World War, but this list has often been challenged, and the most authoritative modern researcher, Kevin Myers of the *Irish Times*, has reduced it by about 10,000. The list contained names of men who were almost certainly not born in

Ireland, but who chanced to be in an 'Irish regiment', or men of Irish descent but not birth who joined up in England or elsewhere, and were registered as 'Irish' after their deaths on the strength of their name, rather than their birthplace.

Myers also suggests reducing the figure for general recruitment from the very high figure of half a million to about 300,000, on two grounds. One is a Royal Irish Constabulary census taken in 1919, which stated that 240,000 men then living in Ireland, North and South, had served in the war. Add to this approximately 40,000 dead, and a notional number of Irish-born men who had served in the war but who in 1919 were not living in Ireland, and one arrives at a minimum figure of 300,000 and possibly a great many more. The second reason for accepting the figure of 300,000, or thereabouts, is that in general First World War fatalities ran at about 13 per cent of enlistment. Regarding 40,000 Irish fatalities as 13 per cent of total Irish enlistment again gives one a recruitment figure for Ireland of just over 300,000.

APPENDIX H

De Valera's St Patrick's Day Speech, 1943

On 14 October 1982 there appeared in the *Irish Times*, under the headline 'Dev's vision of an ideal Ireland', a photograph of the Grand Old Man with his grandson Ruaidhri, taken in 1967. The photograph shows a kindly and interested de Valera seated on some steps, with his young grandson, cheek resting on his fist, plainly listening with complete absorption. The paper went on to quote from the famous speech of 1943:

That Ireland which we dreamed of would be the home of a people who valued material wealth only as the basis of right living, of a people who were satisfied with frugal comfort and devoted their leisure to the things of the spirit – a land whose countryside would be bright with cosy homesteads, whose fields and villages would be joyous with the sounds of industry, with the romping of sturdy children, the contest of athletic youths and the laughter of comely maidens, whose firesides would be the forums for the wisdom of serene old age. It would, in a word, be the home of a people living the life that God desires that man should live.

Index

split into Officials and Provisionals, 35; as working-class movement, 156

Irish Revolutions, 1916 to 1921, inspired by cultural revival, 24

Irish Sweep, *see* Irish Hospitals Sweepstakes

Irish theatre, 142-4

Irish Volunteers, foundation and split with National Volunteers, 35

Irish writers in English, 116-27 *passim*

Irish writers in Irish, 116-27 *passim*, 132-3, 185-6

Iron Age: Celts as Iron Age invaders, 12; Irish still in Iron Age at time of Norman Invasion, 16

James II of England, King, defeat of, 76

Jealousy as national trait, rivalled by many other countries, 169-70

Jesus, women free to accompany Him, 79

Jews, abstemious reputation, 104; references to drunkenness in Old Testament, 105; as propagandists, 170

Kerry, skull types similar to Norwegian, 12; pre-Celtic population, 13; drug offences, 160

Kilkenny Design Centre, 136

Knock airport: cost of, 131; possible savings by cancellation, 157; still safe, 173

Koran, attitude to women, 79

Lament of the wife of Art O'Leary, famous Irish poem, 165

Kegion of Mary, 58, 61

Liffey, celebrated by James Joyce as 'Anna Livia Plurabelle', 165; fish (dingy, languid, temporarily insane, but alive) swimming in, 174

Limerick, scene of general strike in 1919, 34-5, 191-2; drug offences, 160; details of 1919 strike, 191-2

Longford, Earl of, and Gate Theatre

Company, 143

Lynch, Jack, Irish Prime Minister, uncertain role in Northern troubles, 39

MacAlister, R.A.S., on Sheldru, the tinkers' language, 179

McCarthy, Justice, verdict in marital case quoted, 83

MacGrundy, Mrs, 21, 24 and *n*

MacLiammoir, Michael, together with Hilton Edwards, and others, as figures in Irish theatre history, 143-4

MacMaster, Anew, actor-manager, 143

McQuaid, John Charles, Archbishop of Dublin, character, conservatism, 65

'Madame Sin', furore over TV appearance, 51

Maebh of Connaught, Queen, noted for her 'hospitable thighs', 78

Marriage, 75-103 *passim*; under Gaelic Law, 77

Marxist Socialism, 191-4; in 1916, 24-5; influence on IRA, 34ff

Matthew, Father, founder of first Irish Total Abstinence Association, 21

Midnight Court, The, poem by Brian Merriman, 20; as evidence of 18th-century attitude to marriage, 132

Mountjoy Square, once-noble town houses, 166

Muckraker, origin of term, 167

National Association of the Ovulation Method of Ireland, advocates of Billings method of family planning, 92

National Stud, as one of Ireland's glories, 53

Normans, invade Ireland, 17; use of stirrups, 17; establish political authority and English law, 76

Nuns, statistics regarding convents and orders of, 60